Canada: A Very Short Introduction

VERY SHORT INTRODUCTIONS are for anyone wanting a stimulating and accessible way into a new subject. They are written by experts, and have been translated into more than 45 different languages.

The series began in 1995, and now covers a wide variety of topics in every discipline. The VSI library currently contains over 650 volumes—a Very Short Introduction to everything from Psychology and Philosophy of Science to American History and Relativity—and continues to grow in every subject area.

Very Short Introductions available now:

ABOLITIONISM Richard S. Newman
THE ABRAHAMIC RELIGIONS
    Charles L. Cohen
ACCOUNTING Christopher Nobes
ADAM SMITH Christopher J. Berry
ADOLESCENCE Peter K. Smith
ADVERTISING Winston Fletcher
AERIAL WARFARE Frank Ledwidge
AESTHETICS Bence Nanay
AFRICAN AMERICAN RELIGION
    Eddie S. Glaude Jr
AFRICAN HISTORY John Parker and
    Richard Rathbone
AFRICAN POLITICS Ian Taylor
AFRICAN RELIGIONS
    Jacob K. Olupona
AGEING Nancy A. Pachana
AGNOSTICISM Robin Le Poidevin
AGRICULTURE Paul Brassley and
    Richard Soffe
ALBERT CAMUS Oliver Gloag
ALEXANDER THE GREAT
    Hugh Bowden
ALGEBRA Peter M. Higgins
AMERICAN BUSINESS HISTORY
    Walter A. Friedman
AMERICAN CULTURAL HISTORY
    Eric Avila
AMERICAN FOREIGN RELATIONS
    Andrew Preston
AMERICAN HISTORY Paul S. Boyer
AMERICAN IMMIGRATION
    David A. Gerber
AMERICAN LEGAL HISTORY
    G. Edward White

AMERICAN NAVAL HISTORY
    Craig L. Symonds
AMERICAN POLITICAL HISTORY
    Donald Critchlow
AMERICAN POLITICAL PARTIES
    AND ELECTIONS L. Sandy Maisel
AMERICAN POLITICS
    Richard M. Valelly
THE AMERICAN PRESIDENCY
    Charles O. Jones
THE AMERICAN REVOLUTION
    Robert J. Allison
AMERICAN SLAVERY
    Heather Andrea Williams
THE AMERICAN WEST Stephen Aron
AMERICAN WOMEN'S HISTORY
    Susan Ware
ANAESTHESIA Aidan O'Donnell
ANALYTIC PHILOSOPHY
    Michael Beaney
ANARCHISM Colin Ward
ANCIENT ASSYRIA Karen Radner
ANCIENT EGYPT Ian Shaw
ANCIENT EGYPTIAN ART AND
    ARCHITECTURE Christina Riggs
ANCIENT GREECE Paul Cartledge
THE ANCIENT NEAR EAST
    Amanda H. Podany
ANCIENT PHILOSOPHY Julia Annas
ANCIENT WARFARE Harry Sidebottom
ANGELS David Albert Jones
ANGLICANISM Mark Chapman
THE ANGLO-SAXON AGE John Blair
ANIMAL BEHAVIOUR
    Tristram D. Wyatt

Available soon:

For more information visit our website

www.oup.com/vsi/

Donald Wright

CANADA

A Very Short Introduction

OXFORD
UNIVERSITY PRESS

OXFORD

UNIVERSITY PRESS

Great Clarendon Street, Oxford, OX2 6DP,
United Kingdom

Oxford University Press is a department of the University of Oxford.
It furthers the University's objective of excellence in research, scholarship,
and education by publishing worldwide. Oxford is a registered trade mark of
Oxford University Press in the UK and in certain other countries

First edition published in 2020

Impression: 1

Published in the United States of America by Oxford University Press
198 Madison Avenue, New York, NY 10016, United States of America

British Library Cataloguing in Publication Data
Data available

Library of Congress Control Number: 2020934983

ISBN 978-0-19-875524-1

Printed in Great Britain by
Ashford Colour Press Ltd, Gosport, Hampshire

For Harriet and Frances
And for Mohammad, Abdullah, Alaa, Doaa, and Haya

Contents

List of illustrations

List of maps

Map 1. Modern Canada.

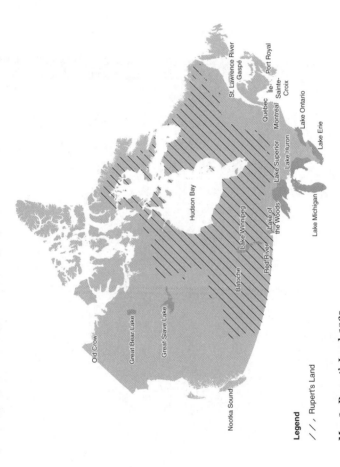

Legend

/ / / Rupert's Land

Map 2. Rupert's Land, 1869.

Introduction

This introduction to Canada begins in Syria. In September 2012 shelling by the Syrian army forced Qassim Albrdan, Manal Hredeen, and their four children to cross the border into Jordan where they registered as refugees with the United Nations. The next couple of years were a blur of camps, apartments, and a new baby, named Haya after Jordan's Princess Haya, a UN Messenger of Peace. Finally, the Albrdans received a telephone call and two weeks later they landed at Toronto's Pearson Airport as part of what Ottawa described as a national project: between 2015 and 2018 Canada accepted over 60,000 Syrian refugees.

Although Canada had shut its doors to Jewish refugees in the 1930s—taking a position of 'none is too many'—it changed course after the Second World War. In the late 1940s and early 1950s Canada accepted 250,000 displaced persons from Central and Eastern Europe; in 1956 it welcomed nearly 40,000 Hungarian refugees; and twelve years later it received 12,000 refugees from Czechoslovakia. Throughout the 1970s, 1980s, and 1990s, tens of thousands of refugees arrived from Uganda, Chile, Lebanon, Laos, Cambodia, Vietnam, Bosnia, and Kosovo. In one year alone, 1979–80, Canada resettled 60,000 refugees from Southeast Asia. Immigrants too have built new lives in Canada: since 1945, millions of people from around the globe, from Austria to Zululand, have immigrated to Canada. In any given year

Canada accepts 250,000 immigrants, a number that is projected to increase to 350,000 in 2021. The overwhelming majority settle in one of the major urban centres—Montreal, Toronto, Calgary, and Vancouver—but even Yellowknife, a city of less than 20,000 people in the Northwest Territories, has an Ethiopian restaurant.

Qassim and Manal knew only two things about their new country when they boarded a second plane: that it was very big and that it was very cold. Flying into Fredericton, a small city of 60,000 people in Atlantic Canada, they contemplated the unfamiliar landscape, its frozen rivers and its endless expanse of trees and snow, and wondered what they had got themselves into. To fly over Canada is to fly over a silent and alien continent, an archipelago of cities large and small separated by impossible distances. Although they didn't know it, Qassim and Manal had asked the Canadian question: what is Canada?

To its critics, Canada is not a real country. It's too large and too diverse and its history is too complicated. Even scholars concede that it's a difficult country to know. At nearly 10 million square kilometres, it stretches across six time zones, east to west, from the Atlantic Ocean to the Pacific Ocean, and south to north, from its border with the United States to the High Arctic. (See Map 1) Only Russia is bigger. Thirty-five million people live in Canada, the vast majority along a thin, southern line near the American border, making it larger than Australia but smaller than California. Most Canadians speak either English or French as their first language, but more than one in five have another language as their first, primarily Mandarin and Cantonese, but also Punjabi, Tagalog, Spanish, and Arabic. Incredibly, 126 different languages are spoken by students in the Toronto District School Board. And although Christianity in general, and Roman Catholicism in particular, still claim by far the most adherents, nearly one million Canadians now observe Ramadan, making Islam Canada's fastest growing religion. In short, Canada is one of the most ethnically, linguistically, and religiously diverse countries on the planet while Greater Toronto may be the world's most diverse city: half of its residents were born outside Canada.

Writer Shani Mootoo captures the immigrant experience of dislocation and integration in 'A Garden of her Own', a short story about a Caribbean woman of South Asian descent learning to navigate her new life in Canada where the land goes on forever and where, as a result, she feels exposed, even naked. Living in a dingy apartment above a busy street in Vancouver, Vijai is terribly lonely: she misses her family, she has no friends, and her husband works long hours. In time, however, she teaches herself a few words in French by listening to the television and she plants a small balcony garden, watching the seeds grow in her new country: while identities may be lost, they can be remade too in Canada's bilingual and multicultural soil.

Because of its size and its diversity, Canada has never had a single national identity. In 1877, just ten years after Confederation, a journalist described Canada as a lost cause and looked forward to its inevitable union with the United States. But the lack of a single national identity is a strength, not a weakness, something that historian Ramsay Cook (1931–2016) understood. Across the length of his career, he resisted the temptation to define Canada. National definitions may be convenient, he argued, but they are incomplete at best and exclusionary at worst. Instead, he encouraged his students to think about Canada as a country that has been made and remade over time, not as a country with an essential identity to be defined, encircled, and defended. Using words like contingent, unfinished, untidy, and *métissage*, or mixture, to describe Canada, he pushed his students to see Canada's history as plural, not singular. Canada, he said, is a country with multiple and sometimes competing identities. And he insisted that Canadian history includes everyone: Indigenous and settler, French and English, men and women, queer and straight, black and white, European, Asian, African, and West Indian. Italian workers and Mennonite farmers, he believed, are as important as prime ministers and business leaders. And while the 17th-century French explorer Samuel de Champlain may be considered the 'Father of New France', it was women, because they had so many children, that ensured the survival of the French language in North America: Catherine Moitié, for example, was just 14 years old when she was sent from France to New France in 1663, but she had eleven children, sixty-five grandchildren, and 344 great-grandchildren.

Similarly, it will be Qassim Albrdan, Manal Hredeen, and their family who fashion a new Syrian Canadian identity and who ensure Canada's ongoing commitment to pluralism. Three months after they arrived, as soon as the snow melted, they received a small plot in a community garden to grow their favourite vegetables and to put down roots, literally and metaphorically.

Ramsay Cook understood something else too: the northern half of North America was never empty. When, for example, King Charles II incorporated the Hudson's Bay Company in 1670 and made it the 'absolute' proprietor of all 'lands, countries, and territories' in the Hudson Bay drainage basin—an enormous sweep of forest, grassland, and tundra across the heart of the continent—he described it as a place 'not now actually possessed'. But the Royal Charter ignored the Cree people who did possess it and who called it *nituskeenan*, our land. At least initially, the relationship between the Hudson's Bay Company and Indigenous peoples was marked by cooperation and mutual benefit: meeting Britain's relentless demand for beaver pelts, Indigenous peoples received valuable trade goods, from kettles to firearms. But the introduction of market forces, alcohol, and disease to the interior of North America cast a long shadow. When Canada purchased Rupert's Land—today northern Quebec, northern Ontario, all of Manitoba, and much of Saskatchewan, Alberta, and Nunavut—from the Hudson's Bay Company in 1869, it was the largest real estate transaction in world history. (See Map 2.) Its original inhabitants, however, weren't consulted. Two years later,

Cree chiefs along the North Saskatchewan River petitioned the lieutenant governor of Manitoba: 'We heard our lands were sold and we did not like it; we don't want to sell our lands.'

Any introduction to Canada must start therefore with the Indigenous peoples who have occupied this land since time immemorial: indeed, the word Canada derives from *kanata*, an Iroquoian word meaning village or settlement.

Chapter 1
Beginnings

The earliest history of North America is not written in the journals of famous explorers or the official dispatches of colonial administrators, but in stone tools and bone fragments, some taken from the Bluefish Caves located high in the Yukon near the First Nations community of Old Crow. Parallel cut marks on a caribou pelvis, made by a stone tool used to deflesh a carcass, indicate that humans occupied the caves as a seasonal hunting camp 24,000 years ago. But how did they get here, when all but a tiny fraction of northern North America was entombed in ice? Almost certainly they crossed the Bering land bridge, or Beringia, connecting eastern Siberia, much of Alaska, and part of the Yukon. A vast, arid grassland that supported a complicated ecosystem of plants, insects, birds, and large mammals, including the woolly mammoth, the giant short-faced bear, and the scimitar cat, all long extinct, Beringia also supported small groups of hunter-gatherers. Following the great herds of caribou and steppe bison—in effect, following protein and fat—they entered a new continent.

When the planet began to warm 18,000 years ago, the slow melt of the ice sheets submerged the land bridge, opened ice-free corridors down and across northern North America, and gave Canada much of its distinctive geography: Newfoundland's Gros Morne channel, Nova Scotia's Bay of Fundy mud flats, southern

Ontario's fertile soil, Georgian Bay's Thirty Thousand Island freshwater archipelago, Saskatchewan's Cypress Hills, Alberta's prairie ponds, and British Columbia's deep, wide river valleys. Perhaps the most distinctive feature is the Laurentian Shield, eight million square kilometres of rocky upland stretching east to west, from Labrador to the Northwest Territories, and south to north, from southern Quebec to the High Arctic. Poet F. R. Scott famously described the Shield as older than love: after all, some of its rocks are four billion years old, as old as Earth itself. Retreating ice sheets wrenched the entire landscape, leaving scarred granite, a thin soil cover, and countless rivers and lakes, including the Great Lakes, Lake Winnipeg, Lake of the Woods, Great Slave Lake, and Great Bear Lake. Hudson Bay was created by the fantastic weight of the ice pressing the Earth's crust into an enormous, deep basin.

As the ice melted, trees followed, their seeds carried on the wind or by birds. It took several thousand years, but the boreal forest—named after Boreas, the Greek god of the north wind—now covers half of the Canadian landmass. A 1690 French dictionary defined *impénetrable* as something that can be neither pierced nor traversed, as in, it added, *les forêts du Canada*. A wide, green, coniferous band of spruce, fir, and pine, the boreal forest is now part of the Canadian imagination. Tom Thomson, whose paintings mythologized the forests of northern Ontario in the 1910s, struggled to get the greens right. In this country, wrote poet Gwendolyn MacEwan, even your dreams are green.

Ice-free corridors allowed the Palaeo-Indians to move south and east, down the Pacific coast, into the Great Plains, eventually reaching the lower Great Lakes, the St Lawrence Valley, the Atlantic coast, and ultimately, the Subarctic and the High Arctic. Adapting to new climates and new environments, Indigenous peoples developed new economies. In the Pacific Northwest, they fished salmon and farmed shellfish, although some groups also hunted whales and sea lions; on the Plains, they relied almost entirely on the plains bison, or the buffalo, for food, clothing, bedding, and tools; and in the northeastern woodlands, they hunted large game, trapped small fur-bearing animals, fished, and gathered berries and edible roots.

Over time, distinct cultures, languages, and social structures emerged. On the west coast, the Haida and the Nuu'chah'nuth were sedentary, hierarchical societies based on heredity and accumulated wealth. They even owned slaves, acquired usually through raids against other Indigenous groups, although individuals could be born into slavery. But on the east coast, the Mi'kmaq were more egalitarian, lived in smaller groups, and moved from their summer fishing spots on the coast to their winter hunting grounds. Chiefs were judged by their ability to lead and to provide, but enjoyed little power over their people, except in war. In the High Arctic, the Inuit lived in even smaller groups, a handful of families really, with no leader or chief, although a headman was common, usually a skilled hunter and conciliator. In the lower Great Lakes, however, the Wendat (Huron) formed a confederacy of four, possibly five, nations in the 16th century, lived in villages of 1,500 to 3,500 people, and relied on agriculture, principally corn, beans, and squash. The Wendat confederacy was also defensive, aligned against the Haudenosaunee (Iroquois) confederacy of five nations south of the lower Great Lakes. Bound together by the Great Law of Peace in the 15th century, the Haudenosaunee confederacy was smaller and more geographically dispersed, but it too consisted of a string of villages that relied on agriculture.

North America was neither outside of history nor empty when Europe 'discovered' it in the late 15th century. It was home to some 500,000 people, belonging to numerous distinct cultures and speaking over fifty languages, but who were connected by elaborate trade routes criss-crossing the continent and who shared a similar cosmology. Despite different rituals, festivals, feasts, and rites of passage, Indigenous peoples believed that humans, animals, and plants enjoyed equal positions and interacted on equal terms, that everything had a spirit, including trees, rocks, and waterways, that the spirit world was as real as the material world, and that it was owed respect, even reverence, through prayers, offerings, and small daily practices. The Nuxalk on the Pacific coast, for example, would not allow their dogs to eat fish bones because they didn't want to offend the salmon spirits.

Contact

The long encounter between natives and newcomers, or contact, happened in different places at different times, earlier on the Atlantic coast, later on the Pacific coast, and yet later again in the interior of the continent and the far north. Some encounters were peaceful, others were violent. Some were fleeting, others led to lasting and reciprocal alliances and trade relationships. But they all pointed in the same historical direction: Indigenous peoples were brought into the market economies of Europe, they experienced cultural change, even transformation, and northern North America was never the same again.

John Cabot wasn't the first European to 'discover' the 'new found land'. That distinction belongs to the Norse who, some 500 years earlier, had attempted, then quickly abandoned, a settlement at L'Anse aux Meadows on the tip of Newfoundland's Great Northern Peninsula. But he was the first to plant a flag. Now understood as a ceremony of possession, his actions mark the beginning of European exploration and settlement of northern North America. According to contemporary accounts, Cabot and his crew made landfall on 24 June 1497 and quickly proceeded to put up a cross and to plant flags in the name of the Holy Father and the King of England. For the next month, Cabot followed the shoreline, almost certainly Newfoundland's northeastern coast. He didn't find a northwest passage to Asia, but he did find something more valuable: an enormous fishery. As news travelled across Europe, Portuguese, Norman, Breton, French, Basque, and eventually English fishers developed both inshore and offshore fisheries. Rich in protein, codfish connected northeastern North America to a hungry Europe and a hungry Europe to northeastern North America.

But what lay beyond its maritime edge? In 1534 the French explorer Jacques Cartier cruised the rocky, ice-wrenched coast of Labrador—in his words, 'the land God gave to Cain'—before reaching what are now Prince Edward Island, northern New Brunswick, and the Gaspé Peninsula. At Gaspé, he encountered Iroquoians, 'the sorriest folk there can be in the world', he said; in fact, they 'go quite naked, except for a small skin with which they cover their privy parts'. Because clothing was a sign of civilization in the European mind, its absence was a sign of primitiveness. Performing his own ceremony of possession on 24 July, Cartier raised a wooden cross in the name of God and of the King of France. But ceremonies of possession were also ceremonies of dispossession, something Donnacona, the Iroquoian chief, intuited. According to Cartier, Donnacona pointed to the cross and then pointed to the surrounding land, 'as if he wished to say that all this region belonged to him, and that we ought not to have set up this cross without permission'.

Five hundred years later, the Indigenous–non-Indigenous relationship is still fraught, especially over land. To protect their territories and their watersheds in the 2010s, Indigenous peoples, from one end of the country to the other, stopped the Northern Gateway and Energy East projects that would have carried Alberta oil west to British Columbia and east to New Brunswick, making yesterday's cross today's pipeline.

In 1535 Cartier followed the St Lawrence River to the Island of Montreal. Of course, he never found a route to Asia. Nor did he find gold. But like Cabot, he remains a key figure in the Age of Exploration, that long century stretching from the late 1400s to the early 1600s: the St Lawrence Valley had been claimed for

France. New names were given to old places and, in the process, reimagined as extensions of France. Essential to any imperial project is the act of naming or, more accurately, renaming. 'This harbour is in my opinion one of the best in the world,' Cartier wrote. 'It was named Port Jacques Cartier.' Giving French names to islands, bays, and peninsulas, in addition to flora and fauna, erased the Indigenous past and remade this corner of the world into a neo-France. Cartography too was important to the imperial project. Using Cartier's maps, which haven't survived, and his detailed reports, Renaissance cartographers produced beautiful representations of northeastern North America that, if geographically fanciful, were ideologically useful, stripping the land of its Indigenous owners.

New France

Fuelled by European rivalry, national glory, religious conviction, collective greed, and individual ambition, France established permanent settlements in the early 17th century. An attempt in 1604 on Île Sainte-Croix in the St Croix River dividing New Brunswick and Maine ended in disaster when half of the men died. Once freed from what Samuel de Champlain called their 'winter prison', a second attempt was made in 1605 at Port Royal in Nova Scotia. If fitful, the tiny colony of Acadia led over time to a permanent French settler society in the region with its own history and its own identity. But it was the founding of a colony, a few buildings really, at Quebec in 1608 that allowed France to build a North American empire: to control entry to the St Lawrence River was to control entry to the continent.

If Champlain understood the strategic logic of Quebec, he also understood that European boats, even skiffs, were too big and too heavy to navigate North America's many waterways. But with the narrow, light, and stable canoes of the Indigenous peoples, he could move, in his words, 'without restraint'. In taking the canoe, France took a continent.

Initially, Quebec was a tiny commercial outpost at the centre of an expanding fur trade. The trade in furs was not a new thing. Seventy-plus years earlier, Cartier had been surprised by the eagerness of the Iroquoians he had met to trade the furs they were wearing until they 'all went back naked'. (Parenthetically, James Cook had a similar experience in 1778 when he encountered Indigenous people anxious to acquire knives, axes, and kettles in what is today British Columbia: indeed, *makúk*, or let's trade, may have been the first Mowachaht word that he heard.) But in the 16th century the fur trade had been limited to the coast and incidental to the fishery. Then everything changed. The sudden popularity of the wide-brimmed felt hat in early 17th-century Europe drove the demand for fur ever higher which, in turn, drove the growth of the fur trade and its extension into the continent. By 1620, 15,000 beaver pelts were traded each year; by 1720, that figure was closer to 200,000 as the trade stretched north to Hudson Bay and west into the prairies; and by 1820, it had reached the Pacific, though by this point the beaver had been pushed to the edge of extinction. If the fur trade almost extirpated beavers, it also largely determined Canada's boundaries, east, west, and north, leading one historian to muse that the aptly named *Castor canadensis* literally gave its life for Canada.

As merchants and their capital entered New France, so too did missionaries and their God. Cartier had reported that the Indigenous people he encountered would be easy to convert and that their god was a fool. Determined to carry the gospel to the New World and prepared to endure impossible privations, the Society of Jesus, or the Jesuits, sent missionaries to Acadia in 1611 and to Quebec in 1625, eventually establishing missions in Wendake, the territory of the Wendat, including Sainte Marie Among the Hurons near the shores of Georgian Bay. Similarly, the Ursuline Order established a convent in Quebec in 1639. At first, the idea of a universal religion didn't make sense to Indigenous peoples who had their own beliefs and their own understanding of the afterlife. Christian proscriptions around sex didn't make sense either, the Montagnais shaman Pigarouich vowing never to give up women or, for that matter, feasts and the belief in dreams. In 1640 Sainte Marie Among the Hurons counted only fifty converts. By the end of the decade, however, there were several thousand Wendat converts, although most who had converted did so in order to secure a preferential trade relationship with the French or to cement an existing one.

If the Holy Gospel was an agent of empire, the real shock troops were foreign pathogens. For example, the Iroquoians that Cartier had encountered in the mid-16th century were gone when Champlain first explored the St Lawrence Valley in the early 17th century, either dispersed by the Wendat and Algonquin looking to dominate the early fur trade or wiped out by disease. It is impossible to overstate the impact on Indigenous peoples of European diseases, especially smallpox, but also measles, mumps, strep, and influenza. As early as 1611 the Jesuit priest Pierre Biard reported that the Mi'kmaq in Acadia were dying. In 1634 smallpox began its pitiless assault on the Wendat, reducing the population from 30,000 to 10,000 by the end of the decade. Both were chapters in a hemispheric tragedy: wherever Europeans went in the Americas, from the 16th to the 19th century, epidemics and staggering death rates followed, turning the narrative of exploration and settlement into a narrative of disease and death.

In 1649 the Haudenosaunee attacked the weakened and divided Wendat, dispersing them from their territory, killing the men, and adopting the women and children to replace their own population, also depleted by war and disease. The Jesuit priest Jean de Brébeuf was captured, tortured, and killed. But was he a Christian martyr? For 350 years that has been the standard line. In 1930 he was canonized and, ten years later, named a patron saint of Canada. But what if his death isn't read as a martyr's death but instead as an Indigenous death? What if he was tortured and killed not as Brébeuf but as Echon, his Wendat name, as an enemy of the Haudenosaunee, not as a defender of the Catholic faith?

Rethinking Brébeuf as Echon compels us to rethink early Canadian history: the Haudenosaunee didn't play a supporting role in a French and Catholic script; they played the lead role in their own script, even if that script didn't have the ending they might have liked.

The non-Indigenous population of Canada, concentrated in a short, thin line from Quebec to Montreal, was just 3,000 in 1663 when the French Crown made it a royal colony and assumed direct control. Its goal was ambitious: to create a settlement colony. Its means were simple: encourage immigrants, especially women. And its success was mixed: French peasants were reluctant to leave France (where they enjoyed land rights) for New France (where the all-but-impenetrable forests had to be cleared, where long winters meant short growing seasons, and where war with the Haudenosaunee carried a terrifying price). Still, enough people were prepared to risk everything, despite Canada's reputation as a country at the end of the world. In 1685 Canada had a French-speaking population of 10,000 and in 1760, when it fell to the British, it had a population of 70,000. A modest number to be sure, but it represented a doubling every generation. At the same time, a new identity had taken root, based on the French language, the Catholic faith, local folklore, customs, and manners, and the land itself. The farmers, artisans, voyageurs, day labourers, merchants, and market vendors in the countryside and in the towns weren't French. They were Canadian, or *Canadien*.

By and large, the *Canadiens* were small-scale, largely self-sufficient peasant farmers whose lives were framed by a system of rights and obligations inherent in the seigneurial system, a feudal system of land tenure unique in colonial North America. The Crown granted large tracts of land to individual seigneurs, or lords, who in turn sub-granted it to individual farmers, or habitants. Stretching away from the St Lawrence River and its tributaries, and backing on to the forest, were long, thin, and rectangular lots that gave each farmer access to fresh water, transportation, and a small woodlot. In return for the right to farm the land, to leave it to his heirs, and even to sell it, the farmer was obligated to pay the seigneur a *cens*, an annual token payment, and a *rente*, a more significant payment in either kind or cash. But the seigneur also had obligations, including the provision of a gristmill and sometimes a court of law to settle minor disputes. And unlike British landlords, he could not evict his tenants and he had to use the courts to collect outstanding payments. In addition to the *cens* and the *rentes* there was the tithe, a payment to the *curé*, or parish priest, set at one-twenty-sixth of the grain harvest.

At least initially, the seigneurial system had obvious advantages because speculators could not hoard land and because families did not need a large down payment to establish a farm. Over time, however, a different picture emerged: a significant portion of the agricultural surplus was given to priests and landlords, making them in effect a local aristocracy and retarding economic development.

If New France was primarily French and Catholic, it wasn't only French and Catholic. There were important Haudenosaunee communities at Kahnawaké and Kanesataké near Montreal and a Wendat community at Wendaké near Quebec. There were a small number of Protestants. And there were slaves, both Indigenous (mostly Pawnee) and African. According to one estimate, there were 2,000 slaves in New France from 1700 to 1760, including Marie-Joseph Angélique, a Portuguese-born African slave, who worked as a domestic servant in Montreal. When her mistress threatened to sell her to the West Indies in 1734, she set fire to her home, a common form of slave resistance, but the wind carried the embers and soon much of lower Montreal was in flames. Poet Afua Cooper imagines Angélique, who was tortured and executed, telling her confessor to 'write down my story so it can be known in history'. Indeed, Angélique is an important and compelling reminder that New France was not only white but also black.

And where yesterday's historians referred to the homogeneity of New France, today's historians understand that it was a multicultural society.

The fall of New France

France and Britain were powerful empires and therefore powerful rivals on both sides of the Atlantic. The War of the Grand Alliance, the War of Spanish Succession, and the War of Austrian Succession meant that New France knew war, preparation for war, and rumours of war. Officially the Seven Years War began in 1756, but unofficially it began in 1754 when the French, British, and Haudenosaunee confronted each other in the Ohio Valley, making it a nine-year war in North America. The stakes were huge: for the French and British, it was control over much of the continent; for the *Canadiens*, it was control over the St Lawrence Valley; for Indigenous peoples, primarily allies of the French but also allies of the British, it was control over their territory; and for the Acadians, once Britain began the deportation of 10,000 men, women, and children from their farms and villages in 1755, it was pure survival.

In 1759 Britain defeated France on a farmer's field less than 1,000 metres outside the walls of Quebec. France capitulated the following spring and, three years later, formally ceded New France, 'quelques arpents de neige', sniffed the French philosopher Voltaire. But to the people who lived there and who had never read French Enlightenment philosophy, New France wasn't a few acres of snow. It was home.

The Battle of the Plains of Abraham lasted just a few minutes but the Battle of the Battle of the Plains of Abraham, fought by historians, journalists, and politicians, has lasted over 250 years. To French Canadian historians, the Conquest was a short- and long-term tragedy that forestalled the normal development of

New France from colony to nation, rendering it a colony interrupted. In the 1960s and 1970s, Quebec separatists insisted that only Quebec's independence could correct the course of history. To English Canadian historians, however, the Conquest didn't alter the basic logic of Canadian history: the development of a transcontinental commercial empire based on a series of staples, or commodities, first fish, then fur, and later timber, wheat, and minerals. If anything, the Conquest had tied Canada to Great Britain, a much stronger commercial and maritime power. Maybe. Maybe not. One thing, however, is clear: the memory of the Conquest has persisted. In 2009 the National Battlefields Commission cancelled its plans to commemorate the 250th anniversary of the Battle of the Plains of Abraham, leading to a churlish editorial in *Maclean's Magazine* lamenting that Canadian history isn't written by the winners but by the whiners, by those separatists who saw the planned re-enactment as yet another humiliation.

In any event, Britain could not do in Canada in 1763 what it had done in Acadia in 1755, meaning it would have to find ways to integrate a large, French-speaking, and Roman Catholic population. The *Canadiens* too had to find ways to live in a new and alien empire. Conflict was inevitable, but accommodation, adaptation, and adjustment shaped, and continues to shape, the relationship between French-speaking and English-speaking Canadians. A defining fact of Canadian politics from the 18th century to the present, it has been called the Canadian Fact: French-speaking and English-speaking Canadians have to coexist.

But what did the Seven Years War and the final defeat of France in North America mean for Indigenous peoples? In a word, disaster. 'Although you have conquered the French, you have not conquered us,' an Ojibwa chief told the British when he insisted that he wouldn't give up his forests, lakes, and mountains. But that is precisely what happened. No longer able to play one empire off against the other, Indigenous peoples found themselves politically marginalized and, despite British promises, unable to defend their territory over the long term.

Artist Robert Houle, from Manitoba's Sandy Bay First Nation, spoke to the themes of marginalization and loss in his 1992 painting *Kanata*, a reinvention of Benjamin West's 1770 painting *The Death of General Wolfe*. Where West depicted Wolfe dying a hero's death for the glory of the British Empire on the Plains of Abraham, Houle decentred Wolfe, draining him, and the men surrounding him, of colour. Adding red and blue panels, one on either side, to symbolize the British and French empires, Houle added red and blue touches to the blanket and the feathers of the Indigenous warrior to symbolize forced assimilation. Ultimately, *Kanata* pushes European history to the edges, brings Indigenous history to the centre, and rethinks early Canadian history as French, British, and Indigenous, making it a powerful contribution to the Battle of the Battle of the Plains of Abraham.

British North America

Following the defeat of New France, Great Britain remade northern North America, through force when necessary, but primarily through immigration, settlement, capital, science, and the law. At the conclusion of the American Revolution in 1783, 60,000 Loyalists sought new homes and new lives in British North America. Loyal to Great Britain, persecuted in the United States, persuaded by the promise of free land, and assisted by the Crown, they settled in Nova Scotia, New Brunswick, Prince Edward Island, Quebec, and Upper Canada (Ontario). In effect, they were the first political refugees in modern history. Some Loyalists were wealthy, but most weren't; some were political, military, and religious elites, but the vast majority were farmers and labourers; some were English, but others were Irish, Scottish, German, and French; some were Protestant, but others were Catholic and even Mennonite; some were Indigenous, allies of the

British during the Revolutionary War; and some were black, both slave and free.

In the late 18th century, Birchtown, Nova Scotia became the largest community of free blacks in North America, the names of its citizens recorded in the Book of Negroes. A 150-page handwritten ledger listing the nearly 3,000 blacks who left the United States for British North America, it included Jack, a 10-year-old former slave who had run away from his owner to sail on a ship named *Hope*. However, Nova Scotia wasn't the hoped-for promised land and in 1792 nearly one-third of the black loyalists left for Sierra Leone in West Africa. And if Nova Scotia, New Brunswick, and Prince Edward Island were not slave societies like Virginia, the Carolinas, and Georgia, they were societies with slaves: according to one estimate, between 1,500 and 2,000 slaves came with their Loyalist owners to the Maritimes. Slavery in the Maritimes, at least until the early 1820s, was enforced by violence and upheld by the law. In 1800 New Brunswick Chief Justice George Ludlow—whose family owned slaves and participated in the Atlantic slave trade—concluded that slavery was legal. For his contributions to the law, the University of New Brunswick named its new law building after him in 1968.

The peopling of Canada continued between 1815 and 1850 when close to one million people crossed the Atlantic as part of the much larger Anglo-Celtic diaspora to Australia, New Zealand, the United States, and British North America. They came from England, Wales, and Scotland, although a majority came from Ireland. In the main, they were Protestant, but a sizeable minority were Catholic. They settled in Newfoundland, transforming it into a settlement colony after nearly 300 years as a seasonal fishery; they found work in the forests of New Brunswick, turning it into a timber colony supplying Great Britain's insatiable demand for wood; and they tried their luck in Quebec, building the Lachine Canal in the 1820s and taking work in Montreal's emerging industrial economy. But most immigrants travelled west to Upper

Canada where land could be acquired and where, in the words of an 1832 emigrant guidebook, a man could be 'the lord and master of his own estate'. Indeed, the notion that land could be measured, parcelled, bought, and sold—and the related promise by the colonial state to uphold property rights—underwrote the great land rush. By mid-century Upper Canada had a population of 950,000. Now Ontario, it is still Canada's most populous province.

In rapid succession, forests were cleared, farms were sown, and market economies were realized across British North America. Printing presses, shipyards, brickworks, tanneries, breweries, distilleries, flour mills, foundries, and even a sugar refinery were established. At the same time, canals were dug and railways were built connecting lumber barons, manufacturers, and farmers to their markets. In the political sphere, reforms were demanded while the prairies, the far north, and the Pacific Northwest were imagined as part of a new transcontinental nation. It was a dizzying pace made possible by the perpetual energy of people, capital, markets, and ideas, including liberty, equality, property, and security. British North America wasn't on the sleepy edge of the Atlantic world. It was drawn into a world alive with movement and revolution and made a part of it.

Politics remained contentious, turning on difficult questions of responsible government, a version of self-government, and the raising and spending of public money. Things came to a head in 1837–8. If they didn't enjoy popular support, the Canadian rebellions—one in Upper Canada (Ontario) and another, more serious, one in Lower Canada (Quebec)—constituted a political crisis. Amplifying the crisis in Lower Canada, moreover, were strong nationalist and republican currents: in the words of one *Canadien*, the queen was a whore. The rebellions were quickly and easily defeated and, in a clear display of the Empire's might, the captured rebels were tried for treason and either fined, executed, or transported to penal colonies in New South Wales and Van Diemen's Land, now Tasmania. Still, Great Britain had a problem. Not wanting to be shut out of the northern half of the continent in the same way that it had been shut out of the southern half, it conceded responsible government to its British North American colonies between 1848 and 1855.

The defeat of the *patriotes* in Lower Canada and the eventual concession of responsible government, however, didn't solve the 'problem' of Britain's Catholic and French-speaking colony where religion, language, and nation animated politics. One solution was assimilation and, to this end, Great Britain united Upper and Lower Canada into a quasi-federal union in 1841, the United Province of Canada, with two sections, Canada East and Canada West. But a vigorous policy of assimilation was never pursued. Today, 23 per cent of Canadians speak French at home. In Quebec that figure is close to 87 per cent.

Confederation

British North America was at a crossroads in the 1860s: it could continue to exist as a string of colonies stretching from Newfoundland to Vancouver Island or it could form a federal union. Having been floated since at least 1839, Confederation was not a new idea, although it never gained momentum, the distances between the colonies being too great. But as railways, telegraphs, and printing presses shrank those distances, the idea of a transcontinental nation became increasingly attractive and viable. Meanwhile, the Northwest—an enormous agricultural frontier representing the promise of Eden—inspired visions of destiny and predictions of settlement. Still, Confederation was by no means unanimous: negotiations were difficult; opponents were determined; and questions of identity were debated, sometimes bitterly. But in 1867 the British North America Act constituted the Dominion of Canada.

A federal union, it consisted of two orders of government: a central, or federal government, and four provincial governments, each order of government sovereign in its assigned powers. To the federal government went, among other powers, defence and currency; to the provinces went, again among other powers, education and hospitals. Although the metaphor of marriage is sometimes used to describe Canada in 1867, divorce is also a useful metaphor. Driving Confederation was political deadlock in the United Province of Canada and the need for its constituent parts to separate one from the other and to become Ontario and Quebec. Union, said a leading French Canadian politician in 1865, was a separation that would allow Quebec to preserve its autonomy and its institutions, especially its church and its language. But if reconstituted along new federal lines, the Canadian Fact—the fact of coexistence between French-speaking and English-speaking Canadians—was still a fact.

In time, more provinces entered Confederation: Manitoba joined in 1870; British Columbia in 1871 with the promise of a transcontinental railway; and Prince Edward Island in 1873 with the promise of better terms, including financial assistance and year-round communications with the mainland. In 1905 Alberta and Saskatchewan entered as new provinces carved out of the old Northwest. For its part, Newfoundland deferred the question to an election in 1869: urging Newfoundlanders not to sever their connection to Great Britain in order to join 'an incongruous and hybrid people'—a reference to Canada's British and French population—the St John's *Morning Chronicle* shouted, 'Let us never change the Union Jack for the Canadian beaver!' (Of course, the *Morning Chronicle* was wrong. Although sovereign, Canada did not cut its ties to the Union Jack: Queen Victoria was still the head of state; acts required royal assent to become law; foreign relations, until 1931, were the purview of Britain; the Judicial Committee of the Privy Council, until 1949, was the final court of appeal; and amendments to the British North America Act, until 1982, could be made only by Westminster.) In the end, the Anti-Confederates carried the day in 1869 and, afterwards, held a mock funeral for the very idea when they interred a coffin labelled Confederation below the high-water mark in St John's. Eighty years later, however, in 1949, it would be the Confederates who, by the slimmest of margins, carried the day when Newfoundland voted in two referenda to join Confederation.

At the federal level, the principle of representation by population was conceded in the lower house, the House of Commons, meaning Ontario and Quebec would have more members of Parliament than New Brunswick and Nova Scotia. However, the principle of representation by region governed the upper house, the Senate, making it, in theory, a house of the regions, an institution in which the smaller, less populated regions would not be overwhelmed by the larger, more populated regions. It didn't work and it hasn't worked: appointed for life—now until the age of 75—and lacking democratic legitimacy, senators proved more loyal to their leaders and their political parties than to their regions and provinces. Mackenzie King, Canada's longest-serving Liberal prime minister and, for that matter, its longest-serving prime minister, appointed 103 senators between 1921 and 1948, 102 of them Liberals. Incredibly, Senate reform has been on and off the national agenda since 1887, leading one historian to call it the longest-running scandal in Canadian politics.

Of course, on 1 July 1867 most people weren't thinking about Newfoundland or the Senate or the constitutional division of powers between the federal and provincial governments. It was a day to celebrate what one newspaper called 'our new destiny'. In cities and towns across the country people gathered for picnics, games, and artillery salutes. True, not everyone celebrated: fearing the loss of New Brunswick's independence and identity, a Fredericton newspaper observed a 'smouldering' discontent. After all, Confederation was never a popular, or a people's, movement.

In the Northwest, a different and more tragic discontent was slowly burning: just a few months earlier, in January 1867, an

1. A haunting photograph from the mid-1890s, 'Last of the Canadian Buffalo' is a visual reminder of what happened on the prairies.

official with the Hudson's Bay Company at Fort Edmonton reported that the buffalo were disappearing (Figure 1). Ten years later they were effectively gone and the Plains Indigenous peoples were making the difficult transition to reserves.

Chapter 2
Dispossessions

Speaking to the House of Commons in 1883, Sir John A. Macdonald confessed that he wasn't sorry that the buffalo had disappeared because, as long as there was hope that the herds would return, it would be difficult to compel the Plains Indigenous peoples to settle on reserves. Describing the Northwest as Canada's inheritance, Canada's first prime minister added that future generations expected nothing less than bold patriotism from this generation. Of course, what Macdonald saw as Canada's trust fund belonged to someone else, a fact that required the federal government to negotiate a series of treaties with the land's original owners.

Negotiating and signing treaties had been the basis of Britain's Indian policy since the late 18th century when the Royal Proclamation of 1763—sometimes called the Indian Magna Carta or the Indian Bill of Rights—obligated the Crown to protect Indigenous peoples from land-hungry and often unprincipled settlers. But in the late 19th century there was a new urgency: the west had to be settled before the Americans could acquire it. Between 1871 and 1877 Canada negotiated a series of treaties in the Northwest—called the numbered treaties—with the Cree, the Ojibwa, the Assiniboine, and the Blackfoot, among others. While the negotiations were two-way, the Indigenous peoples had been dealt a weak hand: intertribal warfare between the Blackfoot and

Cree in the 1860s carried heavy losses; a smallpox epidemic in 1869–70 exacted a grim toll, on the Blackfoot especially, but on the Cree as well; and hunger had reduced some Indigenous groups to eating gophers, prairie dogs, and even mice. A way of life thousands of years old had collapsed. Still, Indigenous peoples saw themselves as equals and the treaties as land *sharing* agreements. Land was not something that could be ceded. But to treaty negotiators, land could be ceded and the treaties were land *surrender* agreements. In the words of Treaty Six, the Indians 'do hereby cede, release, surrender, and yield up' forever 'their rights, titles, and privileges' to their former lands in return for reserve lands, farm implements, livestock, schools, and cash annuities.

The tragedy of history lies not in the treaties themselves but in Canada's failure—and sometimes its refusal—to fulfil its end of the treaties: reserve lands tended to be marginal; farm implements and agricultural instruction were not forthcoming; food rations were parsimonious and, on occasion, withheld; and some government officials, tasked with administering the treaties and overseeing Canada's Indian policy, traded food for sex, in effect forcing Indigenous women into prostitution. A member of Parliament was blunt in 1886: instead of honouring its treaty obligations, Canada had pursued an 'inhuman policy of submission by starvation'.

The Metis

Descendants of Scottish and French traders and their Indigenous wives, the Metis had carved out a place in the plains economy, in the buffalo hunt, and in provisioning the fur trade. But they were rightly worried about settlement. When the Canadian government sent surveyors to Red River (Winnipeg) in 1869 to redraw the region into townships, sections, and lots, the Metis saw their future: dispossession by lines on a map not of their making. Led by Louis Riel—who was French-speaking, Catholic, and Metis—they stopped the surveyors by literally standing on their chains; next, they prevented the lieutenant-governor, appointed by Canada, from entering the territory; and finally, they seized Upper Fort Garry and declared a provisional government. Forcing the government's hand, Riel and the Metis negotiated Manitoba's entry into Confederation in 1870. Tragically, the land rights they had negotiated proved illusory. Overwhelmed by settlers and land speculators, the Metis moved west, to the South Saskatchewan River Valley, where they developed a system of land tenure based on customary, or Aboriginal, title. Unlike the Indigenous peoples, however, they didn't have treaties and were therefore vulnerable.

Events came to a head in the South Saskatchewan Valley in 1885: Riel had returned from the United States where he had been in exile, determined to lead his people a second time but also tormented by messianic delusions that he had been called by God; an intractable federal government refused to negotiate; and violence broke out. Although the Metis had hoped the Cree would join them, very few did. Despite their real grievances, they held to their treaty promises to maintain peace and order. The government responded quickly, crushing the Northwest Rebellion, or resistance as Indigenous people call it, and arresting everyone connected to it, including Big Bear and Poundmaker, two Cree chiefs who had struggled to prevent violence, and One Arrow, also a Cree chief whose participation had been tangential at most. At his trial for treason-felony—which was conducted in English with imperfect translation into Cree, there being no Cree words for traitor, rebellion, or Crown—One Arrow listened to the charges against him: 'knocking off the Queen's hat and stabbing her in the behind'. A confused One Arrow asked the interpreter, 'Are you drunk?' Big Bear, Poundmaker, and One Arrow received three-year jail sentences. Others weren't so lucky: charged with murder, eight Cree and Assiniboine warriors were sentenced to death and executed in a mass hanging before a crowd that had been deliberately assembled from nearby reserves to witness the power and majesty of the law and what can happen when one steps out of line.

Charged with high treason, a more serious charge than treason-felony, Louis Riel was convicted and sentenced to hang. His lawyers had raised the issue of his mental fitness, but Riel refused. In his words, he had acted in self-defence against 'an insane and irresponsible government'.

At the moment of his death, Riel entered Canadian culture as a villain to some, as a martyr to others, and as a recurring figure in history, fiction, poetry, art, sculpture, and even opera. Rehabilitated, vindicated, and versatile, he is Canada's own inkblot test: different people see him differently. He is a Metis who fought for Metis and Indigenous rights; he is a champion of French-language rights in a part of the country that too often dismissed those rights; he is a Father of Confederation and the founder of Manitoba; he is a western Canadian in a country that treated western Canada like a colony; and he is a symbol of reconciliation between Indigenous and non-Indigenous Canadians. In short, he is the atonement for Canada's past sins.

Residential schools

In 2008 Prime Minister Stephen Harper issued an official apology to Indigenous peoples for Canada's role in residential schools; compensation totalling $1.6 billion was paid to nearly 80,000 former students; and, with a mandate to investigate and acknowledge what happened to Indigenous children, families, and communities, the Truth and Reconciliation Commission travelled the length and breadth of the country, gathering the stories of former students. In 2015 it released its much-anticipated report: residential schools were part of a larger policy of cultural genocide.

Residential schools date to New France, although they were tiny and largely a failure: Indigenous peoples did not want to be separated from their children nor did they wish to become French. Indeed, it was not until the 19th century that residential schools took root, first in Upper Canada and, after Confederation, across much of the country, including the far north. Paid for by the federal government and run by the churches, residential schools were, according to the Truth and Reconciliation Commission, 'lonely and alien' places staffed by poorly trained and, in some instances, predatory teachers and administrators. The last residential schools closed in the late 1990s. Describing the system of residential schools as a painful story of destruction in the name of civilization, the Commission also acknowledged that it is a complicated story because some Aboriginal peoples benefited. In all, 150,000 First Nation, Metis, and Inuit students attended residential schools, including Joseph Auguste (Augie) Merasty.

Augie Merasty was just 5 years old when he was sent to a residential school in Sturgeon Landing, Saskatchewan in 1935. The next nine years, he said, were like winter: cold, dangerous, and unending. The goal of St Therese Residential School was the goal of every residential school: assimilation. Indigenous languages were banned, as were Indigenous religious and cultural practices. Catholicism was preached, though rarely practised, according to Merasty: '*Oh, God,* I used to think, *what hypocrisy.*' Although some teachers and staff were kind, others enjoyed inflicting pain, including a sadistic nun and one priest in particular. Violence wasn't exceptional, it was structural: a strap across the hand, a slap across the face, and a smack across the backside, for speaking Cree, for not paying attention, and for failing to form a straight line. The violence was sexual too, pederasts using force and coercion and buying silence with candy or the threat of more force.

Fighting the twin demons of alcoholism and homelessness, Augie Merasty died in 2017, a victim of what has been called Canada's national crime, but also a survivor who led an interesting life as a fisher and a trapper and who succeeded in telling his story. He was 87.

The Indian Act

'I want to get rid of the Indian problem,' Duncan Campbell Scott explained in 1920. 'Our object is to continue until there is not a single Indian in Canada that has not been absorbed into the body politic, and there is no Indian question, and no Indian Department.' As deputy superintendent-general of Indian Affairs, Scott oversaw the Indian Act, the primary document governing Canada's relationship with Indigenous peoples. Passed in 1876, it touched nearly every aspect of an Indigenous person's life, literally from cradle to grave. It instituted Indian bands, defined as a body of Indians, that allowed the federal government to impose a new governance structure of elected band chiefs and elected band councils in an effort to end, or at least bypass, traditional governance models of hereditary chiefs and consensus decision making; it defined who was and who was not Indigenous and therefore determined who got and who did not get status, or the legal recognition as Indian; it stipulated that only men could vote in band elections; it established (until 1960) elaborate rules regarding the federal franchise that entailed the loss of status in return for the right to vote in federal elections; it prohibited bands from mortgaging reserve lands in order to raise capital; and it gave the superintendent-general of Indian Affairs unusually wide powers to administer wills and estates. Until 1951, for example, if a widow was deemed 'not of good moral character', her husband's estate went to his children in equal shares. The Indian Act also touched one of the most intimate decisions a woman can make: any status Indian woman who married a non-status man lost her status, as did any children from that marriage, a rule that did not apply to status Indian men.

Because it could amend the Indian Act without the consent of Indigenous peoples, and because it could make Indian policy by administrative fiat, the federal government could solve the so-called Indian problem on its terms. In 1884 it amended the

Indian Act to ban the potlatch in British Columbia, an elaborate feast and gift-giving ceremony designed to redistribute wealth. To federal authorities, it contradicted notions of private property and patient accumulation. And because it reaffirmed a chief's leadership, it hindered the government's desire to introduce band government. After the 1885 Northwest Rebellion, the government instituted a pass system requiring Indigenous peoples in western Canada to have written permission to travel off their reserve. Although rarely enforced and legally dubious, it remained in existence for over sixty years. In 1914 the federal government again amended the Indian Act, making it a crime—punishable by a $25 fine, a one-month prison term, or both—for status Indians in western Canada to take part in exhibitions, performances, and stampedes while dressed in Aboriginal clothing. Although openly defied, the law nevertheless reflected the government's historical intention, dating back to the mid-19th century, to encourage what it called 'the gradual civilization of Indian tribes'. Or, in a word, assimilation.

The government yet again amended the Indian Act in 1927, this time in response to the formation of the Allied Tribes of British Columbia and its assertion of Aboriginal title: in effect, it now became an offence to hire lawyers for the prosecution of land claims. Ostensibly, the government wanted to protect Indigenous peoples from unscrupulous lawyers. In reality, it didn't want to confront in court the complicated question of Aboriginal title in British Columbia where there were no treaties.

In 1969 the government of Pierre Trudeau released its Statement on Indian Policy, better known as the White Paper: to be an Indian, it argued, was to be apart in law and in the provision of government services. It therefore proposed repealing the Indian Act and shutting down the Department of Indian Affairs. Demonstrating a narrow and incorrect understanding of treaties as simple contracts made obsolete by the modern world, Trudeau actually proposed ending them once the appropriate amounts of twine and gunpowder had been paid. Only sameness of treatment, he insisted, would bring Indigenous peoples into the mainstream of Canadian life, with all of its opportunities and responsibilities. Although the White Paper used the language of diversity, dignity, and citizenship, it effectively restated Duncan Campbell Scott's objective. Of course, Indigenous peoples had no love for the Indian Act and had been successful in pressing change. Eighteen years earlier, in 1951, the federal government responded to their demands when it passed an amendment allowing women to vote in band elections and when it removed bans on the potlatch, the wearing of Aboriginal costumes in stampedes and pageants, and the hiring of lawyers to launch land claims. But Indigenous peoples also understood that, for all its faults, the Indian Act conferred legal status and, ironically, stood between them and assimilation.

Caught in a web of legal coercion, in a country that saw them as a problem that it now wanted to solve by repealing the Indian Act, Indigenous peoples fought back: they weren't the problem, Canada was.

Solving the Canada problem

The federal government quickly shelved the White Paper, but it couldn't shelve Indigenous peoples: with renewed energy, a new generation of Indigenous leaders and activists would solve the Canadian problem in the courts, at the table, and, on occasion, in the streets. From one end of the country to the other, comprehensive land claims were launched; resource deals were negotiated; commissions of inquiry were appointed; historical wrongs were acknowledged; compensation packages were agreed to; and legal decisions were handed down. Using the law—expressed in contemporary human rights and embodied in historical proclamations, treaties, and promises—Indigenous peoples advanced the cause of self-government and the building of nation-to-nation relationships. It has not been painless and there have been missteps, but the arc of history is bending towards reconciliation.

For example, in 1967 the Nisga'a people, led by Chief Frank Calder, renewed a legal challenge that dated back to the 19th century: Aboriginal title to their ancient territory in the Nass River Valley in the northern interior of British Columbia, they argued, had never been extinguished. Of course, the governments of British Columbia and Canada disagreed. Undeterred, the Nisga'a continued to press their case and in 1973 the Supreme Court issued a landmark, if complicated, decision. On the one hand, the Court dismissed *Calder* v. *Attorney-General of British Columbia* on procedural grounds. On the other hand, six of seven justices ruled that Aboriginal title—the right to the land itself—exists in common law. A few months later the government of Pierre Trudeau reversed its earlier position, stating that it was prepared to negotiate. It took nearly thirty years, but in 1999 an agreement was reached by the governments of the Nisga'a Nation, Canada, and British Columbia. Called the Nisga'a Final Agreement, it covered everything from land and resources to governance and compensation. It even included the repatriation of Nisga'a artefacts from the Canadian Museum of History and the Royal British Columbia Museum. And reversing two and a half centuries of appropriation-by-naming in one corner of British Columbia, the province agreed to rename thirty-seven place names in the Nisga'a language, making Greenville, for example, Laxgalts'ap.

If land was a key part of the Indigenous struggle, it was not the only part: pressing their own claims, women who had seen their status taken away now wanted it back. As wives, mothers, and daughters, Indigenous women had played leading roles in Canadian history. In fact, the fur trade depended on their labour: in addition to acting as important go-betweens, or diplomats, between the fur traders and Indigenous peoples, they cooked, cleaned, had children, sewed moccasins, made snowshoes, and prepared pemmican, a mixture of dried meat and animal grease. Not only could pemmican be carried over long distances, as a source of protein and fat, it made those distances possible. Beginning in the late 19th century, Indigenous women entered the labour market, sometimes seasonally, for example in the salmon canneries in British Columbia, but often permanently as well, as domestic servants, hairdressers, nurses, and public health educators.

In 1970 Jeannette Corbiere Lavell was a young Ojibwa woman from the Wikwemikong First Nation on Manitoulin Island in Lake Huron when she married a non-status man. A few months later, she received a letter from the Department of Indian Affairs (today the Department of Indigenous Affairs) informing her that she had lost her status pursuant to section 12(1)(b) of the Indian Act. Adding insult to injury, she also received a cheque for $35 representing her share of the monies held by the Crown on behalf of the Wikwemikong First Nation. Politicized by the 1960s, Corbiere Lavell refused to cash the cheque and instead sued the federal government on the grounds of sex discrimination. The first judge dismissed her suit, noting that she was lucky to have married a white man. Meanwhile, the federal government fought her every step of the way, even forcing her to hold bake sales to raise the necessary funds to fight her case. Taking a narrow view of the equality guarantee in the Bill of Rights, the Supreme Court upheld section 12(1)(b) in 1974: Corbiere Lavell had been treated equally in the enforcement and application of the law, meaning she had not been treated any differently from any other status woman who married a non-status man.

Disappointed but not defeated, Indigenous women went to the United Nations in 1977 when Sandra Lovelace, a Wolastoqiyik (Maliseet) woman from the Tobique First Nation in New Brunswick, argued that her human rights, as guaranteed by the International Covenant on Civil and Political Rights to which

Canada was a party, had been violated when she lost her status after marrying a non-status man. Worried about the financial implications of returning legal status to Indigenous women and their children, the federal government dragged its feet. But Lovelace—who remembered how the nuns spanked her and how they made her feel ashamed to be an Indian—would not be deterred from winning back her legal status and embarrassing Canada on the world stage. At one point in the process the government indicated its intention to amend section 12(1)(b), although it did not offer a timeline. Not one to mince words, Lovelace responded, 'Bullshit!' In 1981 Lovelace won her case at the United Nations and, four years later, the federal government removed the offending section from the Indian Act.

If the federal government was obligated to return or grant status to over 100,000 Indigenous women and their children, the First Nations, or bands, were not obligated to return or grant band membership, a separate legal category that carries benefits. It wasn't only a lack of political will that prevented bands from acting; it was also a lack of housing and employment opportunities on reserves, a sad commentary on the poverty that gripped and continues to grip many First Nations across the country.

The economic, social, and health indicators for today's 1.7 million Indigenous people paint a depressing picture. Unemployment rates are roughly double the Canadian average; the poverty rate for children living on reserves is 60 per cent; and for children living off reserves it is over 50 per cent. Food, water, and housing insecurity are all greater for Indigenous people than non-Indigenous people. Indigenous women and girls are five-and-a-half times more likely to be murdered than non-Indigenous women and girls. Incarceration rates for both Indigenous men and women in provincial and federal prisons are utterly disproportionate: Indigenous people make up 5 per cent of Canada's population but 25 per cent of its federal corrections population, leading one observer to call prisons the new residential schools. A 2014 study

2. In *Ahtolimiye* (She Keeps Praying), 2018, Emma Hassencahl-Perley unwrites the Indian Act and gives it new meaning.

concluded that half of the victims of sex trafficking in Canada are Indigenous women and girls. Finally, Indigenous people are more likely than non-Indigenous people to be obese, have chronic health conditions, and be living with HIV/AIDS. Together, these indicators add up to another heartbreaking reality: the suicide rate for Indigenous people is double that of the general population. For Inuit people living in the far north it is eleven times higher.

Canadian history has been written on the Indigenous body in the form of treaties, broken promises, residential schools, and impossibly high poverty, incarceration, and suicide rates, or in the form of dispossessions large and small. Reclaiming the past and rewriting the future will not happen overnight. As the Truth and Reconciliation Commission acknowledged, reconciliation will be hard and it will take time, there being no magic wand and no single answer. But one thing is clear: the answers will not come from the top down, but from the bottom up. They will come from the Frank Calders, Augie Merastys, Jeannette Corbiere Lavells, and Sandra Lovelaces. And they will come from Emma Hassencahl-Perley, a young Wolastoqiyik (Maliseet) visual artist from Tobique First Nation in New Brunswick. Shredding a copy of the Indian Act, an act of forced assimilation, she attached individual strips to a red jingle dress, the Indian Act now written on her body. Standing in the forest of her people in a dress normally worn at a powwow, an Indigenous cultural celebration, she performs an act of reclamation: the ugliness of the Indian Act has been replaced by the beauty of the jingle dress and her body, now rewritten, is her own (Figure 2).

Chapter 3
Nationalisms

Is Canada one nation? Or two nations? Or even three? Well, it's complicated. In law, it is one nation and only Ottawa can speak for Canada. But in fact, it is three nations: English Canada, Quebec, and First Nations. Complicating things, Newfoundland was a self-governing dominion before it joined Confederation in 1949, meaning it too has a national memory and identity. As a result, nationalism has been a recurring theme in 20th-century Canada. Like Sisyphus, the tragic figure in Greek mythology eternally condemned to roll a large rock up a steep hill, Canada has been condemned to roll the nation up the side of a mountain only to watch it roll back down, making the search for a 'we' and an 'us' both historical and elusive. Although not mutually exclusive, Canada's nationalisms are different and that difference has led to conflict. In the first half of the 20th century, Canada's nationalisms clashed during wartime, during the South African War and the two world wars. In the second half, they clashed during the Quiet Revolution, the Other Quiet Revolution, and the struggle for national recognition by First Nations. That clash was interrupted by moments of violence, but in the main Canada's nationalisms were negotiated through a three-decade constitutional debate over the place of Quebec in Canada, as well as the place of First Nations and Newfoundland.

Historian Ramsay Cook was right: at times, Canada has had too much, not too little, nationalism.

Nationalism and war

Canada's first prime minister was not speaking as a colonial politician when, in 1891, he said, 'A British subject I was born, a British subject I will die.' Sir John A. Macdonald was speaking as a nationalist whose nationalism was no less Canadian for being British. Britishness was not imposed top down from the outside, but came bottom up from the inside, from politicians, journalists, writers, and citizens who, in the last decades of the 19th century and across the first half of the 20th century, celebrated Canada's British past and sang its British destiny. To this end, Queen Victoria was placed on a pedestal, literally and figuratively, from one end of the country to the other, from Victoria, British Columbia to Victoria Junction, Cape Breton. United by a common allegiance to a shared crown, the British Empire imparted a sense of power and linked Canada to a noble mission, or what it believed was a noble mission. But Quebec never got misty-eyed for Queen Victoria or her heirs and successors. Nor did it share English Canada's devotion to the Empire and its mission. It had its own national identity as a French and Catholic nation.

Quebec also understood that the Empire carried military obligations that threatened to divide Canada along linguistic and national lines. When Great Britain went to war in South Africa in 1899, Wilfrid Laurier, Canada's first French Canadian prime minister, had to navigate Canada's different nationalisms. Energized by the enthusiasm of a jingoistic press, English Canada wanted to paint the map red, a reference to world maps that showed the British Empire in red and which hung in every school in the country. But French Canada did not see the South African War as its war and, if anything, sympathized with the Afrikaner republics of Transvaal and the Orange Free State against the

British Empire. Searching for a compromise, Laurier sent volunteers only to South Africa. The vast majority were men, prepared to defend the Empire and its honour with their lives, although a handful were nurses and teachers who wanted to assist the Mother Country and its mission.

Navigating Canada's different nationalisms was infinitely harder when a far greater crisis consumed much of the world in August 1914. William Black Creighton, editor of the *Christian Guardian*, was emphatic: 'We are British!' But Henri Bourassa, editor of *Le Devoir*, asked a tough question: although we refer to 'our Empire', have you 'ever considered how little we Canadians count in that Empire'? The street sweeper in Liverpool and the cab driver in London have more say in the running of the Empire, he said, than seven million Canadians because that street sweeper and that cab driver can vote in British elections. English Canada called him a traitor, but Quebec called him a nationalist. Neither Creighton nor Bourassa could have predicted the enormity of the First World War: 620,000 Canadians enlisted in the Canadian Expeditionary Force; 450,000 went overseas; 61,000 were killed; 172,000 were wounded; and 9,000 returned with what was then called shell shock but what is now understood to have been post-traumatic stress. On the home front and in field hospitals were 3,100 Canadian nurses, nicknamed the bluebirds because of their distinctive blue and white uniforms. One hundred years later, Canadians can remember their service at the Nursing Sisters Memorial in Parliament's Hall of Honour. And on cenotaphs and war memorials in cities, towns, and churches across the country, they can read the names of soldiers who were killed and the places they died: Ypres, the Somme, Arras, Vimy Ridge, Passchendaele, and Amiens.

According to conventional wisdom, Canada came of age in the First World War. And like all conventional wisdom, it contains an element of truth. Even before the war ended, Prime Minister Robert Borden had begun to draw on the language of independence and sovereignty when referring to Canada and the Empire. Still, it is not the only truth because the Canada that emerged from the war was also badly divided, English Canada on the one hand and Quebec on the other. The main wedge? Conscription, or compulsory overseas military service. The election of 1917 had lined up English Canadians who supported Borden's conscription policy against French Canadians who opposed it and there were a lot more English Canadians than French Canadians. To English Canadians, French Canadians were a bunch of slackers, if not cowards; to French Canadians, English Canadians were a bunch of ideologues, if not demagogues. When Borden won the election, the Quebec Legislative Assembly debated, but did not pass, a 1918 motion calling for Quebec's secession from Canada. A few months later, in April 1918, anti-conscription riots in Quebec City left four people dead, 150 people wounded, and a police station burned to the ground. In a show of authority, the federal government responded quickly when it declared martial law, suspended habeas corpus, and imposed a curfew in Quebec City. Although very few conscripts made it to the front, the conscription crisis strained national politics, deepened the divide between Canada's two solitudes, English Canada and French Canada, and tilled the soil for an independence movement to take root.

Newfoundland too went to war when 5,500 men joined up, most in the Newfoundland Regiment. But in less than thirty minutes on the morning of 1 July 1916 at the Battle of Beaumont-Hamel, which was part of the larger Battle of the Somme, much of the regiment was wiped out by German machine guns, or mowed down like sheep according to one of the few survivors. Not a single metre of ground had been gained. Since 1917 Newfoundland has marked 1 July as Memorial Day and many Newfoundlanders wear a small bouquet of forget-me-nots in the same way that many Canadians wear a poppy on 11 November. Indeed, Beaumont-Hamel occupies a sombre place in Newfoundland's cultural and national memory. Moreover, the combined effects of the First

World War, especially the terrible burden of debt, contributed to Newfoundland's bankruptcy in the 1930s and its narrow decision to join Canada in 1949. But 1 July is Canada Day, making it a bifurcated holiday in Newfoundland: in the morning, a service is held at the National War Memorial in St John's, the provincial capital; in the evening, fireworks bring the day to an end. The dual meaning of 1 July in Newfoundland makes it a province with a national memory.

Like the First World War, the Second World War tested Canada's national fault lines. Although autonomous in foreign affairs, there was never any doubt that Canada, as a British country and as a member of the British Commonwealth, would declare war against Germany in September 1939. Mobilizing 1.1 million men and women, it sent troops to Hong Kong, Italy, France, and Holland while German U-boats patrolled the Gulf of the St Lawrence, advancing to within 300 kilometres of Quebec City. It played a key role in the Battle of the Atlantic, keeping open the shipping lanes between North America and Great Britain. It managed the British Commonwealth Air Training Plan, training 130,000 crewmen and women. And it landed at Normandy on D-Day, liberating the Netherlands and, with the Allies, pressing into Germany where the 21st Army Group liberated the Bergen-Belsen Concentration Camp in April 1945. When the war ended, 43,000 Canadians had been killed and another 55,000 had been injured, but Nazi Germany had been defeated. Seventy-five years later, Holland still sends Canada thousands of tulip bulbs every year to say thank you.

To his credit, Prime Minister Mackenzie King both understood and successfully balanced Canada's competing nationalisms. If the problem was conscription, the solution was prevarication: 'not necessarily conscription', he said, 'but conscription if necessary'. For the most part, it worked. When conscription was finally imposed in 1944, the war was almost over and a national unity crisis had been avoided. But that did not satisfy many Quebecers: as one more humiliation in a long list of humiliations, it confirmed their status as a minority. Even a young Pierre Trudeau, who later became Canada's longest-serving French Canadian prime minister, flirted with separatism during the war when he joined a secret society and dreamed of 'Laurentie', an independent French Catholic state.

If the tension between English Canadian nationalism and French Canadian nationalism punctuated Canadian politics in the first half of the 20th century, especially during wartime, it dominated Canadian politics in the second half when Quebec and English Canada redefined their national identities and when Indigenous peoples asserted their own national identity.

The Quiet and Other Quiet Revolutions

Technically, the Quiet Revolution was a series of political and economic reforms implemented by the Quebec government between 1960 and 1966 that remade the province into a modern, bureaucratic, and secular state in the fields of education, health, and social welfare. But the Quiet Revolution was more than a series of political reforms because it also remade French Canadian nationalism into Quebec nationalism, a process that began after the Second World War and lasted into the 1970s. No longer defensive and Catholic, it was now assertive and separatist. Ensuring Quebec's survival—an imperative that stretched back to 1759, the Plains of Abraham, and the Conquest—meant achieving Quebec's independence. In this sense, the Quiet Revolution was not particularly quiet. At the same time, English Canada experienced its own quiet revolution, sometimes called the Other Quiet Revolution, when it replaced its definition of Canada as British with a new definition of Canada as bilingual and multicultural where belonging would be premised not on ethnicity and being of the tribe but on equality and citizenship.

Together, the Quiet and Other Quiet Revolutions remade Canada, making the 1960s and 1970s a period of excitement, experiment, and ferment, of impatience and even violence. Managing Canada's different nationalisms would not be easy when everything was on the table and open to reinvention, including the flag, the key symbol of any country.

In 1964 Prime Minister Lester Pearson announced that Canada would have a new flag in time for its centennial in 1967, one that was distinctly Canadian. The old flag, the Red Ensign, had a Union Jack in the upper left quarter and, as a result, could never speak to French Canadians. A parliamentary committee received 6,000 designs for the new flag, featuring, among other things, beavers, bears, and geese. Some even featured a hockey stick. Yet others combined the Union Jack and the fleur-de-lys in a nod to Canada's British and the French heritage. Writing to the *Vancouver Sun*, however, a group of Indigenous students suggested a raven, a thunderbird, or a totem pole because Canada, they said, is on 'our land'. In the end, the committee selected a red maple leaf on a white field. Although the maple leaf had been used as a symbol of Canada since the mid-19th century and although it had appeared on the uniforms of Canadian athletes competing at international events since the early 1900s, many English Canadians resented the new flag. Describing its red and white design as a nosebleed, they called it a sop to the French. It wasn't, but it was part of the de-ethnicization of English Canada and it marked a key moment in the Other Quiet Revolution.

The pace and direction of change was breathtaking. New writers came into their own, including Leonard Cohen, Mordecai Richler, Margaret Laurence, Alice Munro, and Michael Ondaatje. In 1966 Margaret Atwood published *The Circle Game*, her first major book of poetry. Exploring the universal and the particular, from freedom to snowshoes, it brought a tough and incisive voice to the ongoing conversation about Canada and the meaning of Canada. It also introduced a brilliant writer to the world. Suddenly Canada was interesting. Just a few years earlier, in 1960, writer Hugh MacLennan had explained what Canadian books meant to American readers: 'Boy meets girl in Winnipeg and who cares?' Now a lot of people cared because Canadian writers, aided by Canadian publishers, had interesting things to say about diversity, identity, sexuality, and the accommodation of difference, surely one of the greatest challenges confronting western democracies in the second half of the 20th century. Canadian literature, or CanLit, had become a national and recognizable literature, like American literature or British literature, with its own literary giants, key texts, and recurring themes.

In 1967 Canada celebrated the 100th anniversary of Confederation with a year-long party that included parades, picnics, prayer services, and a 5,000-kilometre canoe race from Rocky Mountain House in the west to Montreal in the east. In Vancouver, 100 girls dressed as candles to form a living birthday cake. In Ottawa, a national prayer service acknowledged Canada's religious pluralism. In Toronto, a young man tossed a hammer through the window of the American Consulate, an expression of rebellious youth and a reminder that English Canada, at least, defined itself against the United States, at that moment escalating its war against Vietnam. Still in Toronto, West Indian Canadians organized the city's first Caribana, a celebration of West Indian culture and music and a reminder that Canada wasn't a white country. And in Montreal, the world gathered for the International and Universal Exposition, or Expo 67. As the host country, Canada enjoyed its moment, emphasizing its material successes and cultural achievements as well as its remarkable diversity (Figure 3).

For its part, Newfoundland shared an Expo pavilion with Nova Scotia, New Brunswick, and Prince Edward Island. When Premier Joey Smallwood—who had negotiated Newfoundland's entry into Confederation in 1949 and who liked to call himself the only living Father of Confederation—visited Expo, he was so impressed by its

3. Expo 67 captured the Canadian imagination, as well as the Newfoundland imagination. On Fogo Island, a world away from Montreal, children painted Expo 67 on their float plane.

celebration of everything modern that he arranged for two pavilions, one from Czechoslovakia and the other from Yugoslavia, to be taken apart piece by piece and reassembled in Newfoundland, one in Grand Falls, the other in Grand Bank. For Smallwood, there was no contradiction between his Newfoundland and his Canadian identities: both were modern and forward looking.

But if the optimism of 1967 was real, it was also marked by apprehension, a point stressed by the Royal Commission on Bilingualism and Biculturalism. Appointed in 1963, the commission travelled the length and width of the country in a desperate effort to understand the urgency of Quebec nationalism and the crisis of national unity. In 1965 it reported that Canada, without fully realizing it, was passing through the greatest crisis in its history. And in 1967 it confirmed what everyone knew when it reported that the federal government was functionally unilingual. In response, Canada passed the Official Languages Act in 1969, declaring English and French official languages and requiring all federal institutions, agencies, and crown corporations to provide services in both languages.

To Quebec nationalists, the Languages Act was too little, too late: the problem, they argued, was Quebec's survival, meaning the solution was Quebec's independence, not official bilingualism. Poet Michèle Lalonde angrily refused to 'Speak White', that is, to speak English, the language of the Magna Carta, Shakespeare, and capitalism. And singer Pauline Julien, who had made a point of not performing at a 1964 gala event for Queen Elizabeth II, now told English Canada that Quebec had only a few years to save itself.

What Lalonde and Julien expressed in words and music, the Front de libération du Québec expressed in violence. Inspired by Cuba's Fidel Castro and Algeria's National Liberation Front, consumed by the prospect of Quebec's independence, and intoxicated by romantic notions of violence, the FLQ never enjoyed popular support, although its violence captured headlines across Canada and around the world. Between 1963 and 1970 it placed over 200 bombs at largely symbolic targets, destroying a statue of Queen Victoria in Quebec City, for example, and injuring twenty-seven people in a much larger explosion at the Montreal Stock Exchange. In October 1970 the FLQ plunged the country into chaos when it kidnapped James Cross, a British diplomat and therefore a representative of, in its words, an ancient, racist, and imperial government. To buy time, Ottawa met one of the kidnappers' demands, permitting the FLQ manifesto to be read on Radio-Canada, the public broadcaster. A mashup of anti-capitalism, anti-Catholicism, and revolutionary cant peppered with historical and contemporary grievances, it called for Quebec's total independence. Next, the FLQ kidnapped Pierre Laporte, a Quebec provincial cabinet minister and, according to the FLQ, a member of the collaborating class.

When asked how far he would go to resolve the crisis, Prime Minister Trudeau responded, 'Just watch me.' Three days later, Canadians watched the federal government invoke the War Measures Act, suspend civil liberties, impose curfews, and send the army into Quebec in an overwhelming display of force. The police conducted some 3,000 searches and detained 497 people without charge, including Pauline Julien. On her release eight days later, a defiant Julien told reporters that prison hadn't been all bad, that she had done calisthenics and got back into shape.

To his supporters, then and now, Trudeau had fought fire with fire. To his critics, again, then and now, he had used a sledgehammer on a fly. Two months later, Cross was freed, but Laporte had been murdered, his body stuffed into the trunk of a car. The immediate crisis was over and the FLQ had been extinguished, although the dream of an independent Quebec was still very much alive in the Parti Québécois, a political party committed to achieving Quebec's independence at the ballot box.

Multiculturalism

The Quebec question may have dominated the 1960s and 1970s, but it wasn't the only question: where do we fit in a bicultural Canada, asked Canadians whose ethnic and racial roots were neither French nor British? Demographically, Canada had never been a bicultural country, a point heard over and over again by the Royal Commission on Bilingualism and Biculturalism. Beginning in the late 1890s, immigration was encouraged not only from Great Britain, but from Eastern and Central Europe, Scandinavia, and Italy: between 1901 and 1931 over three million immigrants arrived in Canada. Most settled on the prairies, taking up the offer of free land in what Canadian immigration agents described as the

Last Best West. By the 1920s Canada accounted for nearly half of the global trade in wheat and flour. Of course, not everyone went to the prairies: the Finns found work in the mines and lumber camps of northern Ontario; the Italians moved to Montreal, Toronto, and Hamilton; and, despite laws restricting their numbers, the Chinese and the Japanese went to British Columbia. In 1931 more than one in five people living in Canada were born outside Canada.

Thirty years later, in the early 1960s, Ukrainian, Polish, and German Canadians rejected biculturalism and the idea of two founding races, French and British. Ukrainian Canadians were especially adamant: had they not founded western Canada as immigrants and farmers, they asked, and had they not transformed it into one of the world's great breadbaskets? A better model, they told the Royal Commission, would be multiculturalism. Japanese Canadians agreed, but, speaking from historical experience, they emphasized racial equality and the need to end racial discrimination. After all, 22,000 Japanese Canadians had been interned in 1942, their property confiscated and sold at fire sale prices. In its report, the Commission acknowledged that no one had suffered more because of the war than Japanese Canadians, even noting the inadequate compensation for their lost property.

Citing the ideal of unity in diversity, the Royal Commission made a series of recommendations to facilitate the full development of Canada's many cultural groups, although it stopped short of describing Canada as a multicultural country, believing that was outside its terms of reference. However, Prime Minister Pierre Trudeau was not bound by the Commission's terms and, in October 1971, he made an important announcement in the House of Commons: although there are two official languages, he said, there are no official cultures. 'Canadian identity will not be undermined by multiculturalism', he argued, because 'cultural pluralism is the very essence of Canadian identity'.

First Nations

In ways similar to Quebec and to English Canada, Indigenous Canada experienced its own revolution in the 1960s and 1970s. At the first public meeting of the Royal Commission on Bilingualism and Biculturalism, writer and activist Ethel Brant Monture, speaking for the National Indian Council, said that she didn't fit in a bicultural Canada and that she had no intention of being forgotten. Later, the Indian-Eskimo Association of Canada questioned the premise of bilingualism, noting that Indigenous languages pre-dated French and English by thousands of years. And at Expo 67 Indigenous people used the Indians of Canada Pavilion to display images of broken treaties, forced religion, and impoverished children, compelling visitors to confront a reality that most didn't know even existed. Meanwhile, the chief of the Tsleil-Waututh First Nation in North Vancouver took Canada's 100th birthday as an opportunity to deliver his Lament for Confederation: how could he celebrate, he asked, when his nation had been written out of history? Refusing to play the Convenient Indian, the Indian who quietly and conveniently disappeared, Chief Dan George would be the Inconvenient Indian, the Indian who not only refused to disappear but who insisted on his rights.

When Chief George referred to his 'nation', he drew on a new and self-confident nationalism—a literary, artistic, political, and national renaissance—taking root in Indigenous Canada. Lee Maracle, a writer and activist and the granddaughter of Chief Dan George, described it as a moment of possibility and hope when Indigenous people started talking about their rights. In 'History Lesson', poet Jeanette Armstrong pictured a mob bursting out of the belly of Christopher Columbus's ship and running madly off in all directions, skinning animals, shooting buffalo, and bringing smallpox, alcohol, and eventually processed food. Sculptor Bill Reid introduced Haida art from the Pacific Northwest to people across Canada and around the world. And Metis writer Maria

Campbell published *Halfbreed*, a powerful memoir about poverty, racism, and violence, although the story of her rape by a police officer when she was 14 years old was removed, not because her publisher didn't believe her, but because he feared that the RCMP would seek an injunction preventing the book's publication.

Embracing the language of decolonization and nationalism, Indigenous peoples now referred to themselves as First Nations. When the Dene issued its 1975 Declaration of Dene Nationhood, declaring its independence and insisting on its recognition as a nation, they understood that the word nation retains more authority and commands more respect than the word band. For its part, the National Indian Brotherhood—which became the Assembly of First Nations in 1982—now talked about the inherent rights of self-determination and self-government. But what did self-determination and self-government mean? There was never a single answer. But one thing was clear: Indigenous peoples intended to negotiate with the federal government on a nation-to-nation basis, making constitutional negotiations more complicated.

The 1980 referendum and the patriation of the constitution

In 1980 Quebec held a referendum on independence, or what Premier René Lévesque called sovereignty association. Quebec, he promised, would achieve sovereignty in some fields—in taxation, for example, and foreign affairs—but it would retain an economic association with Canada that included a common currency. It was an emotional campaign, pitting Quebecer against Quebecer. When Lévesque intimated that Trudeau was not a real Quebecer because his middle name was Elliott, Trudeau shot back. Rejecting the awful and racialized logic of insiders and outsiders, he said that his name was a Quebec name and a Canadian name, and that one didn't contradict the other. After the last speech had been given and the final ballot counted, Quebec had voted sixty–forty against separating from Canada.

In the wake of the referendum, Trudeau launched a process to patriate, or bring home, Canada's constitution from Great Britain with an amending formula and a Charter of Rights and Freedoms. A colonial hangover that made no sense in the 20th century, only Great Britain, a foreign country, could amend Canada's constitution. Although there had been attempts in the past to patriate the constitution, Ottawa and the provinces could not agree on an amending formula, on how, exactly, the constitution should be amended. For example, should Quebec, as the only province with a French-speaking majority, have a veto over future amendments? For that matter, should Ontario, as the largest and richest province, have a veto? The debates were legal and technical, but they were also rooted in competing conceptions of Canada: was it ten provinces or two nations?

Earnest speeches, protracted meetings, and difficult court challenges consumed the national agenda for the next eighteen months, but in November 1981 Trudeau realized what has been called his magnificent obsession when he won agreement from nine of ten provinces to a Charter of Rights and Freedoms, entrenched in the constitution and therefore beyond the reach of governments. It was the reason he had entered politics in the 1960s. He also secured an amending formula that did not give Quebec a veto but instead respected the equality of the provinces.

Quebec refused to sign the new constitution. Instead, Lévesque referred to the night a deal was reached between Ottawa and the other provinces as *la nuit des longs couteaux*, as the night of the long knives when Quebec had been stabbed in the back and left to lick its constitutional wounds. Others remember the negotiations differently and correctly: Lévesque had played his cards poorly and lost. But if the night of the long knives was bad history, it was powerful mythology: Quebec had been humiliated. Lévesque told journalists that the consequences would be incalculable, but no one in English Canada was listening. Most polls indicated that English Canadians welcomed a Charter that included French-language rights, Aboriginal rights, women's rights, and a statement of Canada's multicultural heritage.

On an overcast afternoon in April 1982, Pierre Trudeau and Queen Elizabeth II signed the new Canadian constitution into law in a ceremony on Parliament Hill. For the most part, people cheered, although there were one or two audible boos. And more than one journalist commented on the wind and rain, blowing, symbolically it seemed, from the Quebec side of the Ottawa River. After all, Quebec nationalism had not gone away. Nor had the demand for self-government by Indigenous peoples been met. In other words, Canada's constitutional question remained unanswered.

Meech Lake and its consequences

The next front in what was now a decades-long war to constitutionalize and to reconcile Canada's different nationalisms took place over three years, from 1987 to 1990. By any definition, the Meech Lake Accord was a divisive, even traumatic, moment in Canadian politics. Negotiated behind closed doors, between the prime minister and the ten premiers, in a government conference centre at Meech Lake near Ottawa, the Accord was an attempt to accommodate Quebec nationalism and to secure Quebec's signature to the constitution. Of course, Quebec was legally inside the constitution, but it was symbolically outside the constitution, making its signature the final step in the process of constitutional renewal that had been started in the 1960s.

The Meech Lake Accord, or Meech Lake, or simply Meech, proposed several changes to the Canadian constitution—from the federal spending power and the amending formula to the appointment processes for senators and Supreme Court judges—but its most controversial proposal was the recognition of Quebec as a distinct society. It was a variation on an old theme: because Quebec is not a province like the others, it should not be treated like the other provinces. But no one could agree on what, precisely, distinct society meant. Sociologically and historically, Quebec was (and is) distinct. It was (and is) even a nation: renamed in 1968, the provincial assembly is the *Assemblée nationale*; the provincial flag, the blue and white *fleurdelisé*, is considered Quebec's national flag; and the provincial capital, Quebec City, is officially the *capitale nationale du Québec*. But legally and constitutionally Quebec is a province. For the next three years Canadians received a crash course in federalism, constitutional law, and the amending formula. As the clock ticked down and the pressure increased, English Canadians were told to pass Meech or lose Quebec, that the distinct society clause was the price of Canada. But was it? Many thoughtful people didn't think so. And they objected to the process, to eleven men in suits cutting a deal behind closed doors. Indeed, Prime Minister Brian Mulroney and the premiers never understood that the Constitution and the Charter of Rights and Freedoms didn't belong to them. It belonged to Canadians and its promise of equality rights couldn't be rewritten without their meaningful participation and consent.

Although eleven suits cut a deal, that deal still had to be ratified by Ottawa and by each province. In June 1990, as the deadline to complete the ratification process approached, the country witnessed a remarkable unfolding of events, first in Ottawa, then in Newfoundland, and finally in Manitoba. In his words, Mulroney 'rolled the dice' when he brought the premiers to Ottawa in a deliberate and last-minute effort to maximize the pressure on the hold-out premiers of New Brunswick, Newfoundland, and Manitoba: ratify Meech, he told them, or forfeit the country. New Brunswick's premier caved in. But Newfoundland's premier couldn't be moved. Steel-willed to his supporters but pig-headed to his detractors, Clyde Wells had been consistent in his opposition to Meech, which had been negotiated by his predecessor. A rocky outcrop of unrequited dreams on the absolute edge of North America, Newfoundland required a strong federal government, Wells argued. But Meech Lake threatened to weaken Ottawa, he said, because of the limits it placed on the federal spending power, or its power to spend money in provincial jurisdictions like health and social welfare, as well as in the field of regional economic development. It was a curious inversion of Newfoundland nationalism: committed to Newfoundland's survival, Wells stood up for Canada in order to stand up for Newfoundland.

Wells's decision not to put the Accord to a free vote in Newfoundland's House of Assembly didn't matter because, ultimately, the Accord died in Manitoba. On eight separate occasions in late June, Elijah Harper, an Ojibwa-Cree from Red Sucker Lake First Nation and the first Indigenous member of the Manitoba Legislative Assembly, stood in the Assembly, with an eagle feather in his hand and his long black hair pulled into a pony tail, and said, 'No, Mr Speaker', effectively killing Meech on a procedural technicality.

It was not a decision he took lightly, but it was one he felt compelled to take. Between 1983 and 1987 the federal government had met with First Nations leaders in a series of national conferences in an effort to constitutionalize self-government, but to no avail. Now, Canadians were being asked to write a blank cheque to Quebec in the form of the distinct society clause. For Indigenous peoples, it was too much, especially since the Accord failed to include them in its definition of Canada: 'French-speaking Canadians, centred in Quebec but also present elsewhere in Canada, and English-speaking Canadians, concentrated outside Quebec but also present in Quebec', constitute, according to the Accord, 'a fundamental characteristic of Canada'. In jest, some Indigenous peoples even adopted Meech as a verb, as in, 'I've been meeched', or 'I've been screwed.' On behalf of his people, Elijah Harper did not intend to be meeched: Quebec is distinct, he said, but so too are First Nations.

The death of Meech Lake in June 1990 led to another round of constitutional negotiations, resulting in the Charlottetown Accord. But it was so complicated and far-reaching that Canadians, including Quebecers and most First Nations, rejected it in a national referendum in 1992. Exhausted by an endless series of constitutional talks and occasional crises, Canadians had had enough. But the rejection of Meech Lake was interpreted in Quebec as a rejection of Quebec's national aspirations and, in 1994, voters returned the Parti Québécois to power. René Lévesque had died in 1987, but his comment about the incalculable consequences of the 1981 decision to patriate the constitution without Quebec's support turned out to be prophetic. In 1995 Quebec held a second referendum on sovereignty, again with the promise of some kind of economic association with Canada. The polls said that it would be close. On the night of 30 October, Canadians gathered in living rooms, bars, and restaurants to watch the returns, not knowing how Quebec would vote or what a yes vote might mean. Was Ottawa legally obligated to negotiate with Quebec after a yes vote? If it refused, would Quebec issue a unilateral declaration of independence? And if it did, would the world recognize Quebec as a new and independent nation-state?

In the end, it didn't matter: Quebec voted 50.6 per cent no and 49.4 per cent yes. A near-death experience, Canada had escaped a constitutional crisis by less than 55,000 votes. The premier of Quebec blamed money and the ethnic vote. An intemperate remark that raised difficult and persistent questions about who was and who was not a Quebecer, it confirmed an insight from Quebec poet Marco Micone. In 'Speak What', his 1988 response to Michèle Lalonde's 'Speak White', he wondered where immigrants like him fit in Quebec. The 1995 referendum, moreover, threatened not just the break-up of Canada but the break-up, or partition, of Quebec. Insisting that it had a right to national self-determination, the Grand Council of the Crees held its own referendum, asking the Cree people in northern Quebec if they wished to remain in Canada: 96 per cent said yes, suggesting that Quebec, at the very moment of its independence, would have confronted its own separatist movement. After all, if Canada is divisible, so too is Quebec.

Meech Lake, Charlottetown, and the second Quebec referendum ended what political scientists refer to as mega-constitutional negotiations. By definition protracted and divisive, they have not been restarted since 1995, ending a thirty-odd-year debate. While it is true that Quebec has not signed the constitution, it is also true that Quebec has built a modern, social-democratic welfare state in which citizens can live and work in French, guaranteeing the survival of the French language into the foreseeable future and making Quebec's struggle to achieve its independence successful in everything but name. Its independence movement, which was part of a post-1945 worldwide movement to achieve national independence by former colonies, may be the world's most successful independence movement. Certainly, it was the least violent.

Meanwhile, the struggle by First Nations to achieve self-government had its own timeline. Unwilling to reopen constitutional negotiations after the trauma of Meech and Charlottetown, the federal government publicly acknowledged, in 1995, that the right to self-government already existed in the Charter of Rights and Freedoms, in section 35, which recognized and affirmed 'existing Aboriginal and treaty rights'. It also acknowledged that 'one size does not fit all' when it began the process of negotiating a series of self-government agreements with First Nations across the country on education, health, and social welfare, as well as hunting, fishing, and policing.

At times pressing, at other times dormant, the clash of nationalisms in Canada is the burden of being Canadian. English Canada, Quebec, First Nations, and Newfoundland are distinct and each has its own store of symbols, celebrations, and holidays, making Canada a multinational nation. The penultimate Monday in May is Victoria Day in English Canada but *la Journée nationale des patriotes* in Quebec, or National Patriots' Day, named after *les patriotes* who led a rebellion against the Crown in Lower Canada at the very moment a young Victoria came to the throne in 1837. 21 June is National Indigenous Peoples Day. 24 June is Saint-Jean-Baptiste Day, or *la Fête nationale du Québec*. 24 June is also Discovery Day in Newfoundland and Labrador, marking its 'discovery' by John Cabot in 1497. 27 June is Canadian Multiculturalism Day. And, finally, 1 July is Canada Day.

The Canadian calendar may not be neat and tidy, but it works, in part because Canada has a deep rights-based commitment to equality: as a matter of fact, 10 December is Human Rights Day.

Chapter 4
Rights

To demonstrate their loyalty, some 600 Chinese Canadians served in the Second World War while the Chinese Canadian community organized local campaigns to buy Victory Bonds. Despite legal racism in the form of a 1920 law effectively denying Asian Canadians the right to vote in federal elections and a 1923 law banning Chinese immigration, Chinese Canadians wanted to do their bit and, ideally, win their citizenship rights: victory abroad, victory at home. With support from church groups, labour unions, and sympathetic politicians, Chinese Canadians would win their basic rights in 1947 when the Chinese Immigration Act was repealed and the right to vote in federal elections was returned. Indeed, the rights revolution that swept across much of the post-1945 world also swept across Canada, changing it irrevocably and making it a more just society. Everyone, it seemed, understood that they had rights and that they could claim them, in the streets if necessary, and through the courts when warranted. French Canadians, women, gays and lesbians, visible minorities, Indigenous peoples, and organized labour variously embraced the language of rights and, after 1982, used the Charter of Rights and Freedoms to advance equality. In short, rights talk dominated the sometimes strained conversations between citizens, governments, and courts.

French-language education rights

In many ways, language politics are Canadian politics. And, as often as not, the politics of language have been the politics of schools. In 1838, for example, on the heels of the rebellions in Lower and Upper Canada, Great Britain dispatched Lord Durham to investigate the crisis and he, in turn, dispatched an assistant to investigate the state of education in Lower Canada. Sharing Durham's belief that French Canadians should be assimilated, Arthur Buller remarked that education could be an easy and powerful instrument of 'Anglification': no French schools, no French people. Neither British North America nor Canada ever wielded this blunt instrument, but that didn't mean the schools question was settled. In the late 19th century and across much of the 20th century, in New Brunswick, Manitoba, and Ontario, French-language education rights were ignored by hostile provincial governments, unsympathetic courts, and a cautious federal government anxious to respect provincial autonomy, education being a provincial responsibility under the British North America Act. As a result, Ottawa stood on the sidelines in 1912 when Ontario issued Regulation 17 limiting French-language instruction to the first two years of primary school. Although it was repealed in 1927, Regulation 17 lurked in the wings, in Ontario and across the country. For French Canadians outside Quebec, education was not a matter of legal and constitutional niceties, it was a matter of survival.

The question of French-language education rights became urgent in the 1960s and 1970s when Quebec, the geographic, demographic, and political centre of French Canada, stopped seeing itself as part of French Canada and started seeing itself as the nation of Quebec. In effect, the birth of modern Quebec led to the death of French Canada, an irony not lost on French Canadians. And because Quebec had its own constitutional agenda, French Canadians outside Quebec scrambled to formulate their own. At the top of their list, not surprisingly, were French-language education rights, a demand that stretched back to the 19th century and that recalled the ghosts of Lord Durham, Arthur Buller, and Regulation 17. If they did not get everything they wanted, they got a lot: section 23 of the Charter of Rights and Freedoms recognized the right of citizens to educate their children in French or in English in publicly funded primary and secondary schools, where numbers warranted.

In 1990 the Supreme Court issued an important decision, *Mahe* v. *Alberta*. The facts were straightforward: insisting that French immersion was insufficient, Franco-Albertan parents in Edmonton wanted separate French-language schools; when Alberta said no, the parents sued, arguing that their section 23 rights had been infringed. Not only did the court agree, it gave a generous interpretation to section 23. Accepting that language and culture could not be separated, the judges unanimously concluded that its purpose was 'to preserve and promote the two official languages of Canada, and their respective cultures'. In fact, section 23 was intended, the court said, to correct what it called the 'progressive erosion', or the assimilation, of official language groups. There have been other cases from nearly every province, from Prince Edward Island to British Columbia, but the court's logic has been consistent: language, culture, identity, education, and survival are linked, making French-language schools essential to the future French Canadians outside Quebec. In a 2015 decision the Supreme Court went even further, noting that Canada's commitment to minority language education rights not only speaks to the very character of Canada as a bilingual country, it sets Canada apart in the world.

Canada's commitment to French-language education rights is part of its larger commitment to pluralism. In a country as plural as Canada, difference can be either accommodated or subordinated. Over time, and through trial and error, Canada has chosen accommodation over subordination.

Reproductive rights

The women's movement in Canada in the 1960s and 1970s, sometimes called the second wave, was part of a longer historical struggle for equality. The first wave, in the late 19th century and early 20th century, had focused on social reform, access to higher education, and basic citizenship rights, including the right to vote. Now, against the backdrop of the sexual revolution, the women's movement expanded its focus to include reproductive rights, among other priorities. In 1968 the McGill University Student Union published a *Birth Control Handbook*. Printed on newsprint and bound with staples, it was ordered by student groups across the country, from Dalhousie University in Halifax to Simon Fraser University in Vancouver. Distributed free of charge, supply never kept up with demand. And because it addressed both contraception and abortion, the *Handbook* spoke to the growing movement to legalize abortion.

The federal government amended the criminal code in 1969 to permit an abortion if a therapeutic abortion committee of not less than three medical doctors in an accredited hospital determined that the pregnancy presented a danger to the woman's life or health. Although controversial, it was hardly radical because it merely codified what Anglo-American courts had been saying for half a century: not a single court in Canada, the United Kingdom, the United States, or Australia had convicted a woman for terminating a pregnancy when it posed a risk to her life or health. To the women's movement, the 1969 amendment was limited at best and farcical at worst because abortion was, for the most part, still illegal. A group of women confronted Trudeau in Vancouver, branding him a male chauvinist because his vision of the just society did not include them: abortion isn't a crime, the Vancouver Women's Caucus told him, it's a right. To realize that right, dramatic political action, even confrontation, was required. Someone suggested a road trip. And so, on 27 April 1970,

4. A defining event in Canadian second wave feminism and the historical struggle for abortion rights, the Abortion Caravan drew a line in the sand: there was no going back.

seventeen women from the Vancouver Women's Caucus piled into a couple of Volkswagen vans to begin the long drive to Ottawa. On top of one of the vans was a coffin, used to store luggage and to symbolize the countless women who had died seeking an illegal and unsafe abortion. Impressed by its theatricality as she watched the Abortion Caravan (Figure 4) set out from the Vancouver Court House, activist Cynthia Flood pictured an arrow aimed at the heart, the heart being Ottawa and its callous indifference to women's rights.

In parking lots, shopping centres, and community halls, the women performed guerrilla theatre, distributed leaflets, and spoke to journalists. Eleven days and 4,500 kilometres later, they reached the nation's capital in time for Mother's Day. Joined by 300 women from Toronto, Montreal, and Ottawa, they went to Parliament Hill and demanded a meeting with the minister of health, but he was out of the country. Next they demanded a meeting with the minister of justice, but he was playing tennis.

Finally, they marched to 24 Sussex Drive, Prime Minister Trudeau's residence, but he was at Harrington Lake, his summer residence. Still, the women were permitted to leave the coffin, now filled with coat hangers, knitting needles, cans of Lysol, and a vacuum cleaner, all examples of the desperate means women used to end a pregnancy. Two days later, a smaller group of women entered the public gallery in the House of Commons. Chaining themselves to their seats, they disrupted Parliament with their loud and urgent plea for the right to an abortion. Some members of Parliament got up to leave while others remained seated, booing and jeering, yelling 'whores' and 'sluts'. In the end, Parliament was adjourned and the women were removed. But the movement for abortion rights could not be stopped.

Attention now fell on Dr Henry Morgentaler, a doctor and Holocaust survivor who began to perform abortions at his Montreal clinic in 1969, in clear violation of the law. For the next twenty years, Morgentaler found himself in and out of court, first in Quebec, and later in Ontario and Manitoba where he had opened private clinics in 1983, again in violation of the law. Incredibly, he would be acquitted four times, three times in Quebec and once in Ontario, each acquittal confirming what polling data suggested, that attitudes towards abortion were softening and that Canadians were ahead of the law.

Although a key figure, Morgentaler didn't make the movement. The movement made Morgentaler. Behind him was a large and determined network of women that raised money, lobbied governments, pressured hospitals, and assisted women seeking a safe abortion, providing them with a return bus ticket, a place to stay, a bite to eat, and, when necessary, even childcare. In other words, Morgentaler would not have been possible without organizations like the Canadian Abortion Rights Action League, the Ontario Coalition for Abortion Clinics, and the British Columbia Coalition for Abortion Clinics. Eventually, the Supreme Court entered the fray. And in 1988 it released one of its most important decisions when it ruled that Canada's abortion law violated the Charter of Rights and Freedoms, specifically section 7 guaranteeing everyone 'the right to life, liberty and security of the person'. Justice Bertha Wilson, the first woman appointed to the Supreme Court, argued that the right to liberty included reproductive rights: 'the right to reproduce or not to reproduce', she wrote, is integral to 'modern woman's struggle to assert her dignity and worth as a human being'.

Because nothing compels a hospital to provide abortion services, access to abortion services remains uneven across the country, especially for women living in poverty and for women living in the north or outside major urban centres. Still, there is a rough political consensus: abortion is a right, not a crime.

Gay and lesbian rights

Before the late 1960s and early 1970s, gays and lesbians lived in the closet, unable to come out because of the enormous personal and professional costs, to say nothing of the physical risks. Of course, they had created spaces of their own where they could drink, dance, and cruise, in cafés, bars, and parks, in Halifax, Montreal, Toronto, Winnipeg, and Vancouver. But the fear of being outed was real, especially after the Royal Canadian Mounted Police launched a witch hunt in the late 1950s. Convinced that gays and lesbians employed in the military, the federal civil service, and in its own ranks constituted a Cold War security risk because they could be blackmailed by Soviet operatives, the RCMP began a gay hunt and, by the late 1960s, it had opened 8,000 files on known or suspected homosexuals, almost always men. No evidence of Soviet blackmail was ever uncovered, although careers were ended and lives were ruined. And in what historians describe as a grotesque farce, the federal government even funded the development of the fruit machine, a device that researchers believed could detect homosexuality through the measurement of pupil dilation in men who had been shown homo- and heteroerotic images. Although the fruit machine was cancelled in 1967, the gay purge in the RCMP, the military, and the civil service continued into the 1990s and included women as well as men.

When the federal government in 1969 decriminalized homosexual sex between consenting adults in private, it still viewed homosexuality as repugnant, in the words of the minister of justice. One member of Parliament went further, referring to homosexuals as murderous perverts. Another member predicted that the decriminalization of homosexuality would lead to gay weddings, fewer children, and national suicide. Moreover, homophobia wasn't exclusive to the political centre and the political right. At the height of the October Crisis in 1970, the revolutionary Front de libération du Québec referred to Pierre Trudeau, then a 51-year-old bachelor, as 'Trudeau la tapette', or Trudeau the faggot.

For gays and lesbians in the late 1960s and early 1970s, enough was enough: taking their cue from other rights movements, they began to mobilize. In just a few years, there were organizations from one end of the country to the other, from Vancouver's Gay Alliance Towards Equality to St John's Community Homophile Association. The first francophone gay organization, the Front de libération homosexuelle, was founded in Montreal in 1971. Most groups came and went, others lasted several years, and yet others are still active nearly half a century later. Gay newspapers were published, gay bookstores were opened, and lesbian softball leagues were started. In August 1971 Toronto Gay Action hosted the first gay picnic. A few weeks later, it helped to organize the first gay rights demonstration on Parliament Hill (Figure 5). Demand your rights, speakers told a crowd of approximately 100 men and women, including the right to equal employment and promotion in the civil service, the right to serve in the military, and the right to custody in the event of a divorce.

5. At the 1971 We Demand demonstration on Parliament Hill, gay activists turned the lyrics of 'O Canada' into a statement of gay rights.

Like the Abortion Caravan, the We Demand demonstration is now understood as a turning point in Canada's rights revolution: there was no going back, something Maurice Flood understood as chair of the Gay Alliance Towards Equality (GATE). When the *Vancouver Sun* refused a 1974 advertisement for the *Gay Tide*, a gay newspaper, Flood filed a human rights complaint that was eventually heard by the Supreme Court. In its 1979 decision, the court ruled that the freedom of the press includes the freedom not to carry an advertisement. But three justices wrote a powerful dissenting opinion, arguing that a newspaper—or, for that matter, any business that provides a service to the public—cannot reserve to proprietors the right to decide whom they shall and shall not serve. If GATE lost in the short run, it won in the long run, demonstrating that courts could be a venue for lesbian and gay equality rights, especially after the 1982 Charter of Rights and Freedoms.

Section 15 of the Charter prohibits discrimination 'based on race, national or ethnic origin, colour, religion, sex, age or mental or physical disability'. Gays and lesbians had hoped that the Charter would include sexual orientation. After all, Quebec had become the first jurisdiction in Canada, if not the first jurisdiction in the world, to include sexual orientation in its own Charter of Human Rights and Freedoms in 1977. Nonetheless, gay and lesbian activists would use the Charter's promise of equality to win a series of legal decisions, including *Egan* v. *Canada*. In a complicated 1995 decision on benefits under the Old Age Security Act, the Supreme Court ruled that John Nesbit, James Egan's partner since 1948, did not meet the legal definition of spouse, making him ineligible for spousal benefits. But in a separate and unanimous decision, the Supreme Court concluded that sexual orientation 'is a deeply personal characteristic that is either unchangeable or changeable only at unacceptable personal costs', making it analogous to the enumerated grounds in section 15, to 'race, national or ethnic origin, colour, religion, sex, age or mental or physical disability'. On that note, Canada began to change its laws, extending the same benefits to same-sex couples that it extended to heterosexual couples. But it deliberately stopped short of changing the legal definition of marriage. For lesbians and gays, that wasn't good enough: equality included marriage equality. It didn't happen overnight, but in 2005 Canada became just the fourth country in the world to legalize same-sex marriage.

That a later generation will be compelled to apologize for the actions of an earlier generation may be a truism, but it doesn't rob an apology of its power to heal historical wounds. In 2017 Prime Minister Justin Trudeau responded to the deliberately named We Demand an Apology Network when he stood in the House of Commons to apologize to the Queer community, in all its diversity, for the purge of gays and lesbians from federal agencies. He even apologized for the fruit machine.

Minority rights

Multiculturalism is a very Canadian word, referring to a basic demographic fact: census after census has shown that Canada was, and is, ethnically, linguistically, and religiously diverse. The 2016 census, for example, revealed that more than one in five Canadians were born outside Canada. To this end, Omni Television broadcasts Hockey Night in Canada in Punjabi while the University of Toronto student newspaper, *The Varsity*, publishes an on-line Chinese-language edition. Christianity is Canada's largest religion, but its parishioners come from many ethnic and linguistic backgrounds. The Roman Catholic Archdiocese of Toronto, for example, celebrates mass in thirty-two languages. Canada's seven largest cities—Vancouver, Calgary, Edmonton, Winnipeg, Ottawa, Toronto, and Montreal—are arrival cities, cities where people from around the world arrive with their suitcases and their dreams. But multiculturalism is more than a demographic fact. It is also a value. When a local elementary school hosts a multicultural fair for students and parents, and when a city invites its many different ethnic and religious groups to join its Canada Day parade, that school and that city are saying that they value difference and diversity. That value, moreover, found expression in section 27 of the Charter of Rights and Freedoms, making it the only charter of rights in the world to include multiculturalism: 'This Charter shall be interpreted in a manner consistent with the preservation and enhancement of the multicultural heritage of Canadians.'

Of course, the multicultural heritage of Canadians raises the difficult question of minority rights, especially minority religious rights, which in turn raises difficult questions about accommodation: when is it reasonable, and when is it unreasonable, to accommodate the religious rights of minorities? There is no single answer, although there have been numerous examples. In 1991 the RCMP changed its policy—and its iconic uniform—when it allowed a Sikh officer to wear a turban. In 2006 the Supreme Court overturned a ban that had prohibited a student from wearing a kirpan, a ceremonial dagger worn by Sikhs, in his Montreal school, concluding that it violated his religious freedom and stifled multiculturalism. But just five years later, in 2011, Quebec's National Assembly passed a unanimous motion denying entry to Sikhs who refuse to remove their kirpan, even though Transport Canada allows them to be worn on domestic and most international flights. In 2011 the Conservative government of Stephen Harper banned the wearing of a *niqab*, a head covering that also covers a woman's face apart from her eyes, during citizenship ceremonies when new Canadians take the oath of citizenship. In 2015 the Federal Court of Appeal overturned the ban. Not to be outdone, the Conservative government promised to appeal the decision and it proposed a barbaric cultural practices hotline that would allow Canadians to report acts of barbarism, although it could never explain why 911, the emergency telephone number, was not enough. The Conservatives lost the 2015 election, ending both the appeal and the proposed hotline.

Quebec, in particular, has been divided by the debate over reasonable accommodation, not because it is less tolerant, but because it too is a minority culture. Indeed, it never embraced multiculturalism as a public policy, insisting that the Québécois culture was not one more culture among many. After a series of emotionally charged incidents involving accommodation, Quebec appointed a Consultation Commission on Accommodation Practices Related to Cultural Differences in 2007. Called the Bouchard–Taylor Commission after its co-chairs, Gérard Bouchard and Charles Taylor, the commission travelled across Quebec. A year later, it issued its report, noting that the crisis of accommodation had been overstated by a sensationalist media. Still, it urged authorities and civil servants to accommodate dietary restrictions in hospitals, requests by female patients for female attendants, and the wearing of religious headwear in sports and public institutions. At the same time, it recommended interculturalism over multiculturalism and it pushed Quebec to promote interculturalism as vigorously as Canada promotes multiculturalism. Although interculturalism and multiculturalism emphasize the recognition and affirmation of difference, interculturalism also emphasizes the recognition and affirmation of Quebec's French-speaking core. Combining continuity and diversity, interculturalism, at least on paper, affords a measure of security to Quebecers of French Canadian origins and to Quebecers from ethnic and religious minorities.

Not everyone welcomed the report. And in 2013 a new government proposed a Charter of Values which, among other things, banned religious headwear by state employees, including teachers, daycare providers, and healthcare workers, and which required women to uncover their faces when seeking state services. The Charter of Values never became law, but six years later, in 2019, Quebec successfully passed Bill 21, an Act Respecting the Laicity of the State. Proclaiming Quebec's *laicité*, or secularism, it prohibits the wearing of religious symbols at work for a variety of public service employees, from police officers and midwives to clerks and bankruptcy registrars. Government inspectors, or the secularism police to the law's critics, have been empowered to ensure that the law is followed: although there are no fines, disciplinary measures can be taken.

What are English Canadians and Quebecers really talking about when they talk about the *hijab*, the *niqab*, and the *burka*? Of course, it's not one thing, it's several: gender, religion, difference, identity, tradition, modernity, and belonging. Ultimately, however, they are talking about the nation, and that conversation can be hard. Nations are real, bound by borders and held together by laws. But nations are also imagined, bound by history and held together by a set of traditions, stories, and symbols. To quote Bill 21, 'the Quebec nation has its own characteristics'. Yet those nations, the imagined nations, in English Canada and Quebec, change over time: immigrants arrive; refugees rebuild their lives; different voices emerge; new stories are added; traditions are reinvented; the past is challenged; history is rewritten; and the future is reimagined. In this sense, both English Canada and Quebec are part of an ongoing and difficult global conversation on immigration, movement, and changing definitions of nation, of history, memory, people, and place.

Granted, multiculturalism and interculturalism can be official and sometimes facile self-congratulations, precluding tough questions about racism and racialized poverty. But they share an assumption that is also an aspiration: only when individuals feel secure in their ethnic, religious, and linguistic identities will they accept the ethnic, religious, and linguistic identities of others. That security, moreover, is expressed through rights talk and negotiated through a rights regime.

Indigenous peoples, however, are not immigrants. They are the first peoples, making their rights talk different.

Aboriginal and treaty rights

On the one hand, section 35 of the Charter of Rights and Freedoms is clear: 'The existing aboriginal and treaty rights of the aboriginal peoples of Canada are hereby recognized and affirmed.' On the other hand, section 35 is not at all clear because there is no consensus on what constitutes existing aboriginal and treaty rights, including existing aboriginal and treaty rights to hunt and fish. In short, who controls the hunt? Although the question dates to the late 18th century, there was, and is, no simple answer.

In August 1993 Donald Marshall Jr, from the Membertou First Nation in Cape Breton, Nova Scotia, was charged with three offences: fishing without a licence, fishing during the closed season, and selling eels without a licence. This was not Marshall's first run-in with the law. Tragically, he spent nearly eleven years in prison for a murder that he didn't commit before his release in 1982 and his exoneration in 1990. In any event, Marshall did not dispute the facts, claiming instead that he had a treaty right to fish under the 1760–1 Peace and Friendship treaties between the

British Crown and the Mi'kmaq and Maliseet. The treaties were not 18th-century land surrender agreements in some dusty archive; they were living documents that confirmed his people's right to fish in the present. Following a script, the Crown fought him every step of the way, but in 1999 the Supreme Court held that, yes, Marshall had an existing treaty right to fish in order to earn a moderate livelihood, the modern equivalent of his 18th-century treaty right to trade for necessities, for pots, kettles, axes, and blankets. But in a second decision, the Supreme Court also held that the Crown, through the Department of Fisheries and Oceans, had a right to regulate the fisheries. Mediating Crown rights and treaty rights, the DFO negotiated separate agreements with thirty-four different First Nations in the three Maritime provinces.

If a success story because the agreements brought First Nations into the commercial fishery, it is also a cautionary tale because those agreements also defined, and therefore limited, the treaty right to earn a moderate livelihood by Mi'kmaq and Maliseet peoples. In other words, direct access to the fishery by Indigenous peoples for themselves, their families, and their communities became heavily regulated access to the fishery by a handful of licence holders and their crews. Who controls the hunt, or in this case the fishery? The Department of Fisheries and Oceans and the First Nations, but not, ironically, Indigenous peoples. Through the negotiation process, their treaty right to fish was relinquished in return for licences, boats, traps, wharves, and outbuildings. In effect, the treaty right to fish for everyone became jobs for the lucky few who either got a licence or got hired by someone who got a licence. In this sense, Indigenous and non-Indigenous fishers are treated the same way.

In addition to recognizing and affirming existing Aboriginal and treaty rights, section 35, subsection 2, defines Aboriginal peoples as 'the Indian, Inuit, and Metis Peoples of Canada'. It was an enormous political and legal victory for the Metis, historically the most vulnerable of Canada's Indigenous peoples because they did not sign treaties and because they were not—and still are not—governed by the Indian Act.

Specifically, section 35 (2) allowed the Metis to win their existing Aboriginal rights in a series of legal challenges, including a case on the question of who controls the hunt in Ontario's upper Great Lakes region. In 1993 Steve Powley and his son Roddy Powley shot and killed a bull moose near Sault Ste Marie in northern Ontario but were promptly charged by a conservation officer for hunting without a licence under Ontario's Game and Fish Act. However, the Powleys insisted that they had an existing Aboriginal right to hunt for food as Metis people. To make his point, Steve Powley had attached a handwritten tag to the ear of the moose indicating that he was Metis and that it was to provide meat for the winter. Historically, Sault Ste Marie was located on what historians refer to as the fur trade highway, a long network of rivers, lakes, and portages connecting Montreal to the western interior of the continent. As early as 1761, an observer noted a Metis presence in the area, descendants of European fur traders and their Indigenous wives. Half a century later, a distinctive Metis identity and economy had taken root. As in the Marshall case, the Crown fought the Powleys all the way to the Supreme Court. After all, Ontario had never recognized Metis rights and did not want to recognize them now. But in 2003 the Supreme Court ruled that the Powleys had an existing Aboriginal treaty right to hunt for food. It also ruled that the right to hunt for food was not a blanket right, covering the country from one end to the other, but a site-specific right, applying, in this instance, to the Metis community in and around Sault Ste Marie.

The Powley case, like all Indigenous rights cases, drew on history, confirming another truism, that the past is never past, but instead continues to unfold in the present: in a fascinating footnote, the Powleys' lead counsel was Indigenous rights lawyer Jean

Teillet, the great-grandniece of Louis Riel, who sees her fight for the recognition of Metis rights as the continuation of her great-great-uncle's fight.

Labour rights

The efforts by organized labour to secure its rights are historical, stretching back to the second half of the 19th century and the rise of industrial capitalism. From the 1850s to the 1930s there were over 5,000 strikes, walkouts, and riots, one leading to the next. Some ended in modest gains, others in lasting defeat, but labour never threw in the towel, insisting on higher wages, shorter hours, better working conditions, and collective bargaining rights. Bread and butter issues also competed with talk of revolution and dreams of what might be: in labour halls and beer parlours across the country, radical alternatives to the prevailing economic and political order were debated into the morning light.

Capital wasn't sympathetic, and after the Russian Revolution in 1917 it saw Bolsheviks around every corner and under every bed. Insisting that capitalism was the goose that laid the golden egg, it refused to negotiate, preferring instead to hire thugs, crack skulls, break strikes, and, with a sympathetic state, use the power and majesty of the law against labour leaders who stepped out of line, including James Bryson McLachlan. A legendary figure in labour circles, Cape Breton's 'Fighting Jim' was renowned for his generosity—he once gave away his shoes to a man who needed them more—and for his conviction that capitalism was irredeemable. After a violent confrontation between striking coal miners and the provincial police in 1923, the state set its sights on McLachlan: labour would be tamed one radical leader at a time. Charged with seditious libel, an open-ended and therefore convenient charge, McLachlan was convicted and sentenced to a federal penitentiary, making him, for a few months at least, a political prisoner, convict number U-908.

Undaunted, organized labour continued its struggle to ease a burden of poverty made worse by the crisis of capitalism in the 1930s, when the unemployment rate reached 30 per cent, when women stretched food budgets, took in boarders, and looked to cleaning, sewing, and, in some instances, prostitution as sources of informal but paid work, when children turned to stealing food, wood, and coal to supplement the family economy, and when a desperate federal government created a string of remote work camps across the country that housed 170,000 unemployed men.

Finally, in 1940, after years of political and legal wrangling, the federal government established an unemployment insurance programme, a key part of the emerging welfare state. Four years later, both levels of government, federal and provincial, passed a series of labour codes and trade union acts that protected unions, collective bargaining, and the legal right to strike. And from 1945 to the 1970s, Canada witnessed a Fordist compromise between the state, capital, and labour. Named after industrialist Henry Ford, and marked by mass production, mass consumption, and the legal recognition of unions, Fordism ushered in an era of economic growth and relative labour peace: in return for higher wages, job security, and pension plans, a depoliticized labour movement stopped dreaming of what might be and became instead a partner in the economic and political order. But the economic shocks of the 1970s and 1980s and the declining rate of profitability saw the eclipse of Fordism and the rise of neo-liberalism, a much-used, if not always understood, word. An ideological commitment to markets over people on the assumption that what is good for markets must be good for people, neo-liberalism is also a set of business and management practices, for example, outsourcing, subcontracting, and precarious work, or work that is non-unionized, poorly paid, unskilled, and insecure. As well, neo-liberalism is a rewriting of the social contract between governments and citizens that sees governments of all political stripes preach austerity, roll back the welfare state, peg the minimum wage below the poverty line, reduce welfare benefits, restrict public health insurance plans, and make it more difficult to access unemployment insurance and to qualify for workers' compensation.

Disoriented, and at times reeling, organized labour launched a legal challenge to neo-liberalism. Perhaps, it reasoned, the Charter of Rights and Freedoms had the potential to recast Canadian labour relations in neo-liberal times in the same way that it had recast social relations for women, lesbians and gays, religious minorities, and Indigenous peoples. Its strategy worked because in a series of decisions the Supreme Court entrenched labour rights, to the surprise of many court watchers. In *Dunmore* v. *Ontario* 2001, it expanded freedom of association from an individual right to a collective right when it ruled that agricultural workers in Ontario had a collective right to organize, that they could not be excluded from Ontario's labour relations regime, and that the government had a duty to pass legislation giving agricultural workers the freedom to organize. A year later, in *Retail, Wholesale, and Department Store Union (RWDSU)* v. *Pepsi* 2002, the Court argued that secondary picketing—picketing a site other than the primary worksite, including, in this case, the homes of Pepsi management—was a constitutionally protected right to freedom of expression. *Dunmore* and *RWDSU* set the stage for more legal challenges and more legal victories: labour rights are human rights, an energized labour movement argued. In *Health Services* 2007, the Court confirmed that the Charter protects collective bargaining. Citing the scholarship of labour historians Greg Kealey and Bryan Palmer, the Court noted that collective bargaining is located in Canadian history, gives workers a measure of control over 'a major aspect of their lives, namely their work', and enhances their 'human dignity, liberty, and autonomy'. Eight years later, the Court constitutionalized the right to strike in *Saskatchewan Federation of Labour* v. *Saskatchewan* 2015, concluding that the right to strike is part of the collective bargaining process and is, in Justice Rosalie Abella's words, 'supported by history'.

As one of Canada's great rights champions, Justice Abella understood that history matters, that the historical struggle by working men and women—from their response to industrial capitalism in the late 19th and early 20th century to their showdown with neo-liberalism in the late 20th and early 21st centuries—was not for nothing. Although some scholars see the glass half-empty because the constitutionalization of labour rights does not help the majority of workers because the majority of workers are not unionized, other scholars see the glass half-full because the constitutionalization of labour rights is part of Canada's historical and ongoing commitment to equality.

Although it has been used by equality-seeking groups, the Charter of Rights and Freedoms did not give Canadians their rights. Those rights were the result of long and often difficult struggles, some dating back to the second half of the 19th century, others to the second half of the 20th century, a point not lost on Adrienne Clarkson. As Canada's governor general 1999–2005, Clarkson reminded Canadians that she had arrived as a refugee from Hong Kong with her family in 1942, when Chinese people couldn't immigrate to Canada and when Chinese Canadians couldn't vote in federal elections. But times change, things get better, and what was unimaginable in the 1940s, a Chinese Canadian woman governor general, is now part of the Canadian story and a powerful symbol of the rights revolution.

In her 2014 Massey Lectures, Canada's most prestigious lecture series, Clarkson drew on her personal experience as a refugee to talk about citizenship as an idea and as a legal category across time and space. At one point, she noted that immigrants to Canada, before they become citizens, are 'permanent residents', whereas immigrants to the United States, before they become citizens, are 'resident aliens'. The difference between permanent residents and resident aliens, she intimated, is the difference between Canada and the United States.

Chapter 5
Borders

At 8,891 kilometres, it's the world's longest undefended border, a fact taught in every elementary school in the country. Meanwhile, Canadian politicians routinely invoke it as a symbol both of mutual friendship and of Canada's sovereignty because they know that the Canadian–American border is also psychological, that it exists in the national imagination, especially the English Canadian imagination, and that this border, the psychological border, must be defended. Speaking to an American audience in 1969, Prime Minister Pierre Trudeau therefore asserted Canada's sovereignty when he referred to the undefended border. He then added, in a now famous quip, that living next to the United States is like sleeping with an elephant: no matter how even-tempered the beast is, 'one is affected by every twitch and grunt'.

He was right: like the French fact and the multicultural fact, the American fact has shaped Canadian history.

Learning to live together

Canada's relationship with the United States dates to the late 18th century when British North America had to learn, sometimes the hard way, how to share a continent with a rarely easy, often difficult, and sometimes truculent republic that believed God and nature had ordained that it would span the entire continent.

Disputes, border raids, and even war punctuated the early relationship. Although the War of 1812 lasted just two years, it saw the Americans, the British, and the Canadian militia fight a series of battles at sea and on land. In 1813 the Americans attacked York, now Toronto, looting homes, setting fires, and, as a trophy of war, taking the wooden mace, a symbol of the Crown's sovereignty, from the Legislative Assembly. A year later, the British attacked Washington in retaliation, setting fire to government buildings, including the White House, and forcing the American leadership to flee. In the end, both sides claimed victory: the United States had won its claim to the territories west of Ohio while British North America had repelled an American invasion.

Because Canadians have invested the War of 1812 with national significance, they don't like to be told that the invasion was indifferently led and ultimately feeble. Why let facts get in the way of a good story, in this case a national story? Calling it Canada's war of independence, writers, journalists, and politicians have turned General Brock, Laura Secord, and Tecumseh into national heroes and usable symbols of patriotism and loyalty. Yet Brock was a British officer defending British interests, not a proto-Canadian. Secord may have undertaken a dangerous 30-kilometre journey across the Niagara frontier, in what is today southern Ontario, to warn the British of an American attack, but she did not turn the tide, let alone save the country. And Tecumseh, the great Shawnee chief, did not care about the fate of British North America but he did care deeply about the fate of Indigenous peoples in the Ohio Valley when he fought with the British against the Americans. Two hundred years later, in 2012, Canadians marked the war's bicentennial with earnest speeches, commemorative coins, and re-enactments while Brock, Secord, and Tecumseh were given a new shine: they fought for Canada.

In many ways, the War of 1812 was an exception because the Canadian–American relationship, across the 19th century, was characterized by treaties, agreements, compromises, and deepening economic integration. One of the first items of business was the border itself. The Treaty of Paris that ended the American Revolution in 1783 also established the border between British North America and the United States, but words on paper were not the same thing as lines on a map: was there really such a place as the North West Angle of Nova Scotia and where exactly was the source of the St Croix River? It took difficult surveys through impossible borderlands, as well as negotiations and the threat of a third Anglo-American war in the 1830s, before the 1842 Webster–Ashburton Treaty finally confirmed the border from the St Croix River separating New Brunswick and Maine in the east to Lake of the Woods in the west, now on the border of Ontario, Manitoba, and Minnesota. But what about the western border? An 1818 agreement determined that it wouldn't follow natural features but run instead along the 49th parallel from Lake of the Woods to the Rocky Mountains, although it would be another three decades before the last stretch to the Pacific was agreed to in the 1846 Oregon Treaty. But the border still had to be surveyed, a difficult and expensive task that saw British, American, and Canadian teams of astronomers, engineers, and labourers cut wide paths on either side of the line and literally drive iron stakes into the ground between 1872 and 1874.

Not everyone was happy. To some, Great Britain had given away too much. To others, the United States didn't get enough. And while there were occasional calls by American jingoists to fulfil America's manifest destiny and annex British North America once and for all, annexation was never a real threat. The United States may not have liked the idea of a hereditary monarchy on its northern border, but it was largely inoffensive and certainly not worth the price of invasion. According to one historian, the real lesson of the Canadian–American border is not how long it took to negotiate but how innovative the process had been: in agreeing to negotiation, in submitting to arbitration, and in avoiding war, the British, Americans, and Canadians made an important contribution to modern international relations.

Maybe. But for the Plains Indigenous peoples, the border defied common sense, contradicted their experience, cut across their land, and denied their ancient patterns of use and occupation: the prairies couldn't be cut in half. At least initially, the Indigenous peoples simply ignored the border. But for their own reasons, Canada and the United States began to exert control, restrict movement, enforce the law, and deport Indigenous peoples to one side or the other: actually, the prairies could be cut in half and by 1900 the border was largely, if not perfectly, secure.

Writer Thomas King captures the arbitrary reality and the different meanings of the 49th parallel in his short story 'Borders'. When an Indigenous woman attempts to drive across the Alberta–Montana border to visit her daughter, the American border agent, swaying side to side like a cowboy, asks her citizenship. 'Blackfoot', she says. Turned back, she is asked the same question by the Canadian border agent and she gives the same answer. For the next few days, she and her son are stuck between the two sides, forced to sleep in their car in a borderland that had been negotiated well over 100 years earlier by men indifferent to Indigenous peoples and carved out of the prairies by yet other men armed with sledgehammers, stakes, and instruments for measuring angles and distances. And continuing the process of semiotic imperialism that began with Jacques Cartier in the 16th century, lakes and mountains were named after members of the survey teams, their Indigenous names replaced by Cameron Lake and Anderson Peak.

Living together

Canada was naturally wary of the United States, a far larger and more powerful country. In 1867 the population of Canada was just 3.4 million, barely one-tenth that of the United States, while its industrial output was tiny compared to its southern neighbour, at that moment on the cusp of a transformation that would see it become the world's leading industrial nation. Moreover, simple economics—in this case, the economies of scale—meant that American factories could produce shirts, shoes, domestic wares, industrial parts, and everything else under the sun for less, driving down the cost per unit. To protect Canadian manufacturing, Canada implemented a system of protective tariffs along the Canadian–American border in 1879. Like a theological debate, the tariff debate in late 19th-century Canada was lengthy, arcane, and emotional. Wrapping themselves in the flag and calling their tariff policy the National Policy, proponents linked high tariffs to Canada's survival as a separate country in North America, although opponents liked to remind anyone who would listen that higher tariffs meant higher prices for consumers and farmers. On the one hand, the National Policy worked: Canada's manufacturing sector, located principally in central Canada, grew year over year and decade over decade. But, on the other hand, it led to branch plants: to get around Canada's tariffs, American corporations opened subsidiaries, or branch plants, on the Canadian side of the border but kept their head offices on the American side. And tariff wall or no tariff wall, American capital developed Canada's early mining, pulp and paper, and petroleum sectors. A stable democracy that sat on some of the world's largest deposits of minerals, stands of timber, and reserves of oil, Canada was both a safe and profitable place for American capital. By 1914 one-quarter of American foreign direct investment was in Canada.

During the First World War and throughout the interwar years, Canada and the United States continued down the road of cooperation and integration, the continental pull of trade and finance exerting a quiet but powerful logic. But it wasn't only the logic of continentalism that deepened Canada's dependence on the United States. It was also Britain's weakness. Because Great Britain did not have the capacity to lend money to Canada, it effectively forced its former colony into the arms of yet another former colony. The key date? July 1915. One historian has described it as a 'critical' month in Canadian history: at the very moment Prime Minister Borden was in London to attend a meeting of the British cabinet—a measure, surely, of Canada's stature—his minister of finance was in New York—cap in hand—to negotiate a $45 million loan from J. P. Morgan & Co. London still mattered politically, but Wall Street had replaced the City as Canada's key lender. Confirming its deepening relationship with the United States, Canada opened an embassy in Washington in 1926, at first calling it a 'legation' and its ambassador a 'minister' because Great Britain, until 1931, retained ultimate authority over Canada's foreign affairs. But the point had been made: Ottawa would speak directly to Washington, not through London.

The Second World War saw a series of wartime agreements between Canada and the United States, including the Permanent Joint Board on Defence, an advisory board on North American defence established in 1940. Eighty years later it still convenes and still makes recommendations. In the equally important field of trade, a complicated agreement was reached in 1941 that all but erased the border for raw materials and component parts for munitions and equipment. For the duration of the war, it turned the continent into a cross-border munitions factory. There was a lot of handwringing about what this meant for Canadian sovereignty, but the argument was compelling: Canada and the United States may be two countries, but they are one continent with linked economies. Indeed, annual trade statistics didn't lie: Canada and the United States enjoyed one of the largest and fastest growing trade relationships in the world. That trade relationship included a large and growing arms trade, especially after Canada accepted a 1946 Permanent Joint Board on Defence recommendation that Canadian and American forces become interoperational in terms of weapons and equipment and in terms of training, tactics, and signalling. To be clear, American forces didn't Canadianize. Canadian forces Americanized.

Meanwhile, officials on both sides of the border negotiated a comprehensive free trade agreement in 1948. It wasn't a radical idea. It may have made economic sense. But the prime minister quietly pulled the plug, fearing the agreement's implications for Canada's sovereignty and for Canada's soul, for, in other words, the actual border and the psychological border. He would sooner fly to the South Pole, he said, than he would sign a free trade agreement with the United States. A political war horse who had been in politics forever, Mackenzie King remembered the election of 1911 and the fight over free trade, or reciprocity as it was then called. His party, the Liberal Party, supported reciprocity, but it was defeated and he lost his seat when voters were told that reciprocity in trade meant reciprocity in murder rates and that American murder rates were much higher. When it was over, the Conservative Party's war cry had carried the day: 'No truck or trade with the Yankees.'

Although free trade would have to wait, one thing was clear: connected by geography and history, Canada and the United States had become allies and trading partners. Even the War of 1812 had been symbolically forgiven a few years earlier when President Roosevelt ordered the return of Ontario's historic mace which had been held by the United States Naval Academy as a trophy for 121 years.

Canada and the Cold War

A macabre fifty-year nuclear standoff between the Soviet Union and the United States, the Cold War drew Canada closer to the United States. Conscious that it was a junior partner, or an errand boy to critics of American leadership in the Cold War, Canada sought safety in numbers in the international arena. Multilateral organizations like the British Commonwealth of Nations (now the Commonwealth of Nations), the North Atlantic Treaty Organization, and especially the United Nations would provide Canada with opportunities to cultivate different alliances, to assume different roles in the world, and to offset the United States. Neither a superpower nor a minor power, Canada could be a middle power, that is, an honest broker and a helpful fixer on the world stage.

The first conflict of the Cold War—and therefore the first test of collective security—occurred on the Korean peninsula in 1950 when North Korea attacked South Korea. Suddenly, Canada found itself fighting a war in East Asia. Officially, it was a UN war. But unofficially, it was an American war. In all, 26,000 Canadians served in Korea: 516 were killed and another 1,200 were injured. When it ended in a stalemate in 1953, Canada withdrew its troops, leaving historians to debate the war's meaning. To some, it indicated Canada's willingness to follow the United States wherever it went. To others, it indicated Canada's commitment to the principles of multilateralism and collective security. In fact, it was both: Canada did not have a lot of cards to play when its key ally was also the leader of what was then called the Free World, but it played its cards well in the corridors of power, establishing a reputation for diplomacy at the United Nations.

That reputation served Canada in 1956 when Great Britain, with France and Israel, attacked Egypt in response to Egypt's nationalization of the Suez Canal, a vital transportation link connecting Europe to the oil fields of the Middle East. An ill-thought military action by a fading empire, Britain's reckless behaviour threatened to escalate into a much larger conflict involving the United States and the Soviet Union. Although well versed in gunboat diplomacy, the Americans were not pleased and, like everyone else, desperately wanted a way out. Led by Lester B. Pearson, its extremely able secretary of state for external affairs, Canada crafted an exit strategy when it pushed the creation of a United Nations Emergency Force, or a peacekeeping force, that would occupy the canal zone, separate the belligerents, and give diplomats the space to find a peaceful solution. It was a remarkable moment: for a few weeks in the fall of 1956, Canada played the lead role in a global drama. A year later, Pearson received the Nobel Peace Prize.

The Suez Crisis and Pearson's leadership ushered in a new era in Canadian foreign policy: for the next four decades, Canada contributed to every UN peacekeeping mission, in the Middle East, Africa, and Southeast Asia. Incredibly, Canada still maintains a small number of peacekeepers in Cyprus as part of a UN operation that began in 1964. Because it fit with Canada's self-understanding as a middle power, peacekeeping even became part of the Canadian identity, distinguishing Canada from the United States and reinforcing the psychological border: Americans make war, but Canadians make peace. Celebrated in books and sanctified in an Ottawa monument, peacekeeping is now a national symbol. In 2008 the government named 9 August National Peacekeepers' Day: on that day in 1974, nine Canadian peacekeepers were killed when their aeroplane was shot down near Damascus by Syrian forces. Canada's dedication to peacekeeping isn't rhetorical. But nor is it the whole story. Across the length of the Cold War, Canada's obligation to NATO was much larger both in terms of service men and women on the ground and in terms of the percentage of the defence budget it consumed. And among countries contributing to UN peacekeeping missions in 2019, Canada ranked fifty-ninth, behind France, Spain, and Germany, but ahead of the United States.

Canada's historical and ongoing service to the UN has been likened to a national religion, but its faith in multilateralism did not change the fact that its primary foreign relationship was bilateral, not multilateral. And that relationship continued to deepen in the 1950s and 1960s. Built in the mid-1950s to warn of a Soviet attack across Canadian airspace, a series of shared radar lines—the Pinetree Line, the Mid-Canada Line, and the Distant Early Warning Line, or DEW Line—stretched west to east across Alaska and Canada. In 1957 Canada and the United States launched NORAD, the North American Air (now Aerospace) Defence Command, a fully integrated continental air defence command headquartered in Colorado and led by an American commander and a Canadian deputy. Familiar questions were

6. Founded in 1960, the Voice of Women protested nuclear weapons as Prime Minister John Diefenbaker (top) entered the House of Commons in 1961.

asked by Canadian nationalists worried about Canada's sovereignty and by peace activists, including the Voice of Women, worried about Canada's militarization (Figure 6).

Things came to a head during the 1962–3 Bomarc missile crisis. Placed in silos in North Bay, Ontario, and La Macaza, Quebec, as part of a NORAD agreement, Bomarc missiles were American-made anti-aircraft missiles that were effective only with nuclear warheads. The Canadian government had agreed but then equivocated. At one point, the missiles were loaded with sand bags. The Americans were furious. In the end, it took a general election and a new prime minister to resolve the crisis, but in 1963 Lester Pearson agreed to house nuclear weapons on Canadian soil under the ultimate authority of NORAD. To his critics, the irony was too much: hadn't Pearson won the Nobel Peace Prize just a few years earlier?

The Cold War, like all wars, had a domestic front: Canadians were told to build bomb shelters and were encouraged to take up civilian defence, although very few did. Fatalistic, Canadians understood that any nuclear attack would be final, making emergency measures futile. In 1955, Halifax staged an evacuation drill but more cars were seen entering the evacuation zone than leaving it. The Royal Canadian Mounted Police, however, could not afford to be fatalistic. Indeed, it took Canada's national security very seriously when it spied on Canadians. Political policing was not new—it pre-dates the Canadian nation-state—but the Cold War gave it a renewed emphasis: if there were security threats, always broadly defined, they would be found. Civil servants, filmmakers, gays and lesbians, labour militants, immigrants, professors, peace activists, and feminists were screened, some closely, as part of a national security state. Moreover, the RCMP developed closer relationships with MI5, the British security service, and with the FBI, the Federal Bureau of Investigation. And Canada became a part of the Five Eyes, a signals intelligence spy network that included Britain, Australia, New Zealand, and the United States.

Across the Cold War, Fortress North America was built agreement by agreement, radar station by radar station, missile silo by missile silo, and intelligence file by intelligence file. It wasn't an actual fortress, but to Canadian nationalists worried about Canadian sovereignty it felt like one.

From *Lament for a Nation* to free trade

Angered by the missile crisis and convinced that Canada had become a colony of the United States, professor and writer George Grant published *Lament for a Nation* in 1965. Now a classic in Canadian non-fiction, it spoke to English Canada's border anxieties when it mourned the end of Canada as a sovereign state. And it turned the rumpled philosopher into the darling of nationalists everywhere for his critique of the American empire and his unsparing assessment of a homogenized continental culture premised on greed, consumption, and the conquest of nature. The border, he said, had become a mere formality, if not an anachronism.

Lament for a Nation was part of a wave that washed over much of, but certainly not all of, English Canada in the 1960s and 1970s. Disgusted by American excesses in Vietnam and shocked by the racial violence in American cities, English Canadian writers, artists, musicians, professors, and journalists succumbed to anti-Americanism, a disease of the intellectuals. Writing sixty years ago, historian Frank Underhill diagnosed it as an episodic national neurosis: every twenty or thirty years since the early 19th century, he said, British North America and later English Canada has worked itself into a fevered state. It came in many forms—in books, music, and art—but the point was always the same: the Americans are coming! The Guess Who, a Winnipeg rock band, depicted the United States as a dangerous temptress—'she gonna mess your mind'—in its 1970 hit 'American Woman'. Reaching number one on the Billboard Hot 100, its references to war machines and ghetto scenes left little to the imagination. Not to be outdone, a series of books was published across the 1970s—from *Silent Surrender* and *Close the 49th Parallel* to *Sellout* and *Takeover*—that urged Canadians to resist the new Romans.

Actually, an essay and poetry collection published in 1968 had taken *The New Romans* as its title when it invited Canadian writers to address the United States. Dorothy Livesay remembered an incident of everyday racism in New Jersey that, thirty years later, still haunted her. Margaret Laurence connected the grotesque violence in Vietnam to the tragic police shooting of a 12-year-old black boy in Detroit. And Michael Ondaatje pictured a Vietnamese baby, its head split open like an unlaced tennis shoe. In his introduction, poet Al Purdy made a fascinating, if unintentional, confession: although he had invited Quebec writers to contribute, he found few takers. Quebec had never fretted over the United States in the way that English Canada had, something Purdy didn't understand. Ottawa, not Washington, was its concern. René Lévesque, who founded the Parti Québécois in 1968 and became Quebec's first separatist premier in 1976, always said that he felt more at home in the United States than he did in English Canada where the burden of history—of the Conquest and everything that stemmed from it—got in the way.

For their part, politicians and policy makers were not immune to Canadian cultural and economic nationalism. A few years earlier, in 1957, Ottawa had created the Canada Council for the Arts to fund artists, writers, musicians, and dancers. Now, in the early 1970s, it established an elaborate set of rules requiring radio and television stations to broadcast a minimum amount of Canadian content, or Can-con, although what, exactly, makes content 'Canadian' has been a difficult question to answer. Then, in quick succession, the government created the Canadian Development Corporation to develop Canadian-controlled companies in the private sector; it established the Foreign Investment Review Agency to review foreign investment and to ensure that it was in Canada's interest; it launched the Third Option, a trade initiative to reduce Canada's southern exposure by increasing its western and eastern trade relationships with Europe and Asia; and it set up Petro-Canada, a state-owned oil company. Meanwhile, the oil shocks of the 1970s pushed questions of energy and energy security to the top of the political agenda. In 1980 the government introduced the National Energy Program, a far-reaching set of policies that, among other things, aimed to stabilize oil prices and increase Canadian ownership in the oil industry.

The election of a Progressive Conservative government in 1984 signalled a new direction in Canadian–American relations. Prime Minister Brian Mulroney came from the private sector and never understood English Canada's anti-Americanism: the United States was Canada's most important ally and its largest trading partner, not some new Rome. Inspired too by the ideological and economic revolutions of Margaret Thatcher and Ronald Reagan, he distrusted public ownership, government regulation, and protectionism in the same way that he trusted privatization, free markets, and trade liberalization. After the election, he told a Wall Street audience that Canada was open for business, adding that he was more concerned about the Canadian economy than he was about Canadian nationalism. To this end, he dismantled the Canadian Development Corporation; he shelved the Third Option; he scrapped the National Energy Program; and he gave the Foreign Investment Review Agency a new name and a revised mandate. Investment Canada, he promised, would facilitate, not review and certainly not hinder, foreign investment. Few Canadians noticed and, if they did, they didn't care. But when Mulroney initiated trade talks with the United States that led to a comprehensive free trade agreement, Canadians suddenly cared. A lot. True, the idea of continental free trade had been on and off the table since the 1850s, but no sooner would it be revived than it would be rejected. However, this agreement was different. Running to well over 1,000 pages with appendices and schedules, it eliminated most tariffs, reduced non-tariff barriers, or subsidies, and included a dispute settlement mechanism. Still, it would have to be put to the electoral test. Fought over free trade, the election of 1988 may have been loud and at times shrill, but the choice was clear: free trade, yes or no?

The Progressive Conservative Party argued that it was a simple trade agreement and reminded Canadians that Canada had signed, much to the long-term benefit of Ontario's economy, the 1965 Automotive Products Trade Agreement, better known as the Auto Pact, a sectoral free trade agreement for cars and car parts. According to one historian, the United States got the short end of the stick when it was out-negotiated by Canada in 1965. President Lyndon Johnson famously told the Canadian ambassador that the United States had been screwed.

The Liberal Party and the New Democratic Party (NDP), a progressive, left-of-centre third party, responded that sectoral free trade was one thing but comprehensive free trade was another, that it was the thin edge of the wedge and would lead to the border's disappearance. Nonsense, said the Conservatives. It was a simple treaty that could be cancelled with due notice. A simple treaty? Hardly, countered the Liberals and the NDP, because once implemented it would be difficult, if not impossible, to undo. Meanwhile, a visceral anti-Americanism infected the debate. Free trade meant American crime rates, American gun laws, and American healthcare. It even meant American wars and Canadians being drafted to fight in Nicaragua and El Salvador. Calling Brian Mulroney the head waiter at the White House, Liberal leader John Turner in effect called him a weakling, adding that he would defend Canada, a country where hospitals check your pulse before they check your credit card. It was a powerful rhetorical punch. Created in 1966 after years of debate and planning, Canada's publicly funded, universal, and comprehensive healthcare system had become a national symbol, like hockey and maple syrup, and had been used repeatedly to distinguish Canada from the United States.

In a memorable appearance before a parliamentary committee considering free trade, writer and feminist Margaret Atwood stole the show when she argued that Canada had done as well under the United States as women have done under men: 'About the only position they have ever adopted toward us, country to country, has been the missionary position, and we were not on top. I guess that's why the national wisdom vis-à-vis Them has so often taken the form of lying still, keeping your mouth shut, and pretending you like it.'

Although the majority of Canadians voted for the Liberal Party and the New Democratic Party, meaning they voted against free trade, Canada's electoral system rewards the party with the most seats and the Progressive Conservative Party won the most seats. Moreover, Quebec voted overwhelmingly Conservative, ensuring Brian Mulroney's victory. Their national identity on the line,

English Canadian nationalists who had been intellectually and politically sympathetic to Quebec nationalists and their aspirations since the 1960s now felt a deep sense of betrayal: *Et tu, Québec?* But they failed to understand that English Canada's survival had never registered in Quebec, a nation more concerned about its own survival: from its perspective, free trade was a good thing, opening up new markets and strengthening existing ones for *la garde montante*, Quebec's new guard of young and dynamic business leaders. Although not in power, the Parti Québécois believed that, in the long run, it would weaken Quebec's dependence on English Canada and facilitate Quebec's independence.

A done deal, the Free Trade Agreement came into effect on 1 January 1989. Five years later, it was expanded to include Mexico. There was some opposition to the North American Free Agreement, but nothing like the opposition to the Free Trade Agreement. Interestingly, it was a Liberal prime minister who signed NAFTA into law, such was (and is) the ideological consensus between Canada's two main parties. Recognizing Canada's reliance on access to American markets, even the NDP has made its peace with free trade and, in 2019, supported the United States Mexico Canada Agreement, a revised version of NAFTA. In short, Canadians have come to terms with free trade: if it didn't lead to the economic promised land, it didn't usher in American crime rates either and no one was drafted to patrol the streets of Managua or fight in the rainforests of San Salvador.

9/11

The terrorist attacks of 9/11 left the United States bruised and enraged. From the outset, Canada expressed its unwavering support, both officially when 224 US-bound flights were diverted to Canadian airports and unofficially when Canadians opened their homes to 33,000 stranded American passengers, from British Columbia to Newfoundland and Labrador. Three days later, 100,000 Canadians gathered for a public vigil on Parliament Hill in Ottawa.

In the immediate aftermath of 9/11, the United States closed the border for the first time since the War of 1812. Images of a 36-kilometre line-up of trucks at the Windsor–Detroit crossing were a sober reminder of the border's importance to Canada's economy: in 2001 85 per cent of Canada's exports went south; 25 per cent of America's exports came north; and a staggering $1.3 billion dollars in trade goods crossed the border every day. Although the border was reopened within a couple of days, it was clear that the United States meant business: the Patriot Act, America's anti-terrorism legislation passed just weeks after 9/11, contained a section called 'Protecting the Northern Border' which increased the number of border agents, tightened border crossings, and committed $100 million to expand and improve border technology.

In response, Canada had to demonstrate that it too meant business, that it took terrorism and border security seriously. It could not afford to be seen as soft, especially after some American officials and journalists asserted that the 9/11 terrorists had entered the United States via Canada. They hadn't, but Canada quickly passed a series of Acts that gave the Canadian security establishment new powers of surveillance and detention, that allowed airlines to provide personal and confidential passenger information to foreign authorities, and that dramatically increased funding for border security. On cue, some Canadians wondered what 9/11 meant for Canadian independence and Canadian sovereignty. When the discussion turned to visa convergence, that is, the convergence of Canadian and American visa requirements for tourists, students, and temporary workers entering either Canada or the United States, those same Canadians became even more outspoken. Also on cue, other Canadians replied that the United States was Canada's best friend and that musing about Canadian independence and sovereignty was thinly veiled anti-Americanism. Caught in the middle, the government had to dance the Continental Two Step, meaning it had to get close to its dance partner but not too close: visa convergence never happened, although visa cooperation did when Canada rewrote some of its visa requirements along American lines. As more than one scholar has pointed out, the economic imperative of protecting North American supply chains and keeping the Canadian–American border open is also a political imperative.

Although important and ongoing, conversations about the border and border security were overtaken by conversations about the war on terror and Canada's role in it. A NATO country, Canada accepted the NATO principle of collective defence: an attack against one is an attack against all. To this end, it committed troops in October 2001 to Operation Enduring Freedom, America's war against the Taliban government in Afghanistan and the al-Qaeda terrorist network it harboured: Canada was at war. In October 2001 Parliament affirmed its support for Canada's service men and women in their defence of freedom and democracy against terrorism by a margin of 213 to 10. A fluid mission, Canada's role in Afghanistan changed over time and lasted much longer than anyone could have anticipated. Initially, Canada provided security, intelligence, and supply services in the Persian Gulf and it sent special operations forces to Kandahar, a dangerous province in a dangerous region. In 2003 it provided security in Kabul, the Afghan capital, as part of the International Security Assistance Force, a UN-authorized, NATO-led mission. In 2005 it committed to taking on a much larger and much tougher combat assignment in Kandahar. And in 2011, it returned to Kabul to train the Afghan army and police. Called a 3D war—defence, development, and diplomacy—Canada both fought a war and built a peace through diplomatic initiatives, humanitarian relief, reconstruction projects, and public health schemes, for example, a vaccination campaign against polio. When Canada's mission finally ended in 2014, 40,000 Canadian soldiers had served; 158 had been killed; and $18 billion had been spent. But the Afghan government was precarious; the Taliban hadn't been eradicated; and opium production proceeded apace. By any index, Afghanistan was still broken and probably unfixable.

Because of its bilateral responsibility to the United States and its multilateral responsibility to NATO and to the United Nations, Canada did not have a choice: the doctrine of forward security—that security threats must be confronted politically and, if necessary, militarily, at their source—compelled Canada to join the larger international community in Afghanistan. Yet if Canada did not have a choice, it did have a confused public: why is Canada in a landlocked country in Southwest Asia? That confusion found expression in a May 2006 parliamentary vote: 149 members of Parliament voted to extend the mission; 145 members voted not to extend it. Just five years after the *Globe and Mail* had shouted that now was the time to 'let loose' on terrorism, words like expensive, endless, and futile competed with freedom, democracy, and security to describe Canada's deployment.

Forward security, however, did not compel Canada to join the coalition of the willing in Iraq in 2003, a war that lacked the legitimacy of the United Nations. Prime Minister Jean Chrétien understood that the Bush Doctrine, the doctrine of pre-emptive strike, was the exact opposite of multilateralism, the cornerstone of Canada's post-1945 foreign policy. And in a clear example of military policy driving foreign policy instead of the other way around, he also understood that, after decades of underfunding, Canada's military did not have the capacity to be in two places at once. And yet if there was disappointment from south of the border, there was no retribution, despite predictions of Washington's lasting displeasure.

The 2002–3 Iraq debate was about war and peace and Canada's role in the world, but it was also about the Canadian–American border. Canadians rightly worry about that border, a site of trade and trial, but George Grant's lament was ultimately misplaced. The actual and psychological borders are neither formalities nor anachronisms: they separate two very different countries. Bilingualism, multiculturalism, a woman's right to choose, and universal healthcare are public policies, but they are also values that reflect Canada's identity and its commitment to equality.

Of course, nothing can change the fact that the United States is an imperial power or the fact that Canada is a middle power dependent on American power. Against this backdrop, Canada must constantly weigh the reality of bilateralism against the promise of multilateralism and vice versa. In 1970 the government of Pierre Trudeau identified the problem that all Canadian governments confront: how to live 'distinct from but in harmony with' the United States, 'the world's most powerful and dynamic nation'. It could have been written in 1783, 1812, 1867, 1945, 1963, 1988, or 2001, a point President George W. Bush acknowledged in 2004 when, to the knowing laughter of a Halifax audience, he admitted that sleeping next to an elephant isn't easy.

Three years later, Bush made it even more difficult when he insisted that the Northwest Passage is an international waterway (Map 3).

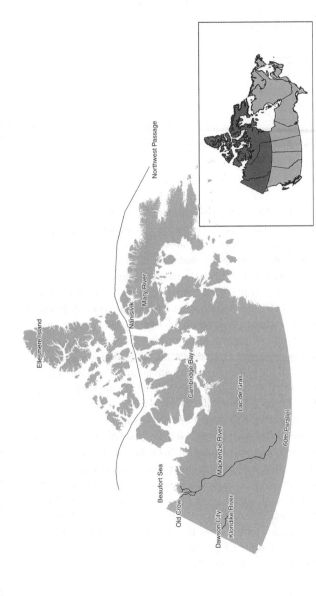

Map 3. Canada north of the 60th parallel.

Chapter 6
Norths

Located just 750 kilometres from the North Pole, Ellesmere Island is the most northern point in Canada and the tenth largest island in the world. The Inuit call it *Umingmak Nuna*, or Muskox Land, after the herds of muskoxen that roam its plateaus and that were essential to their survival on the northern margins of North America where temperatures can drop to −60° Celsius and winds can exceed 140 kilometres per hour. In the 19th century, in the age of empire and polar exploration, Ellesmere Island entered the British world. Although it had been 'discovered' in 1818 and then named in 1852, after Francis Egerton, first earl of Ellesmere, it wasn't until the British Arctic Expedition in 1875–6, led by Capt. G. S. Nares, that its eastern and northern coastlines were mapped, or that its deep fjords, cut by ancient glacial spillways and enclosed by steep cliffs, were charted. New names were given to old places; a flag was planted; 'God Save the Queen' was sung; and Ellesmere Island was claimed for Great Britain. But Britain, concerned that the United States might challenge its Arctic claims, had other plans for Ellesmere Island and, for that matter, the entire Arctic Archipelago: by an 1880 Order in Council, it quietly transferred its North American territories and possessions to its dominion and, just like that, Canada became a circumpolar nation. The Toronto *Globe* reported that Canada now extended from ocean to ocean to ocean.

Consisting of 36,000 islands and covering 1.4 million square kilometres, the Arctic Archipelago is difficult to comprehend. Northrop Frye, a literary scholar and maybe Canada's most important thinker, recalled how, as a schoolboy in the late 1910s and early 1920s, he would learn his geography lessons on old Mercator maps that distorted Canada's north, inflating its size and making it seem much larger than it really was. Describing the north as an immense and looming ghost, he was haunted by how the maps just ended at the top of the page, leaving only a void. Canadians have been struggling to fill that void—to define it and give meaning to it—since the late 19th century because, if it's easy to locate Ellesmere Island on a map, it's paradoxically difficult to locate the north. Where, exactly, does the south end and the north begin? North of the 60th parallel separating the Yukon, the Northwest Territories, and Nunavut from British Columbia, Alberta, Saskatchewan, and Manitoba? Perhaps. But that is a political line, not a climatic or physiographic line. Does the north begin in cottage country north of Toronto? In the late 19th century, it was defined as an instant north, a place to escape the enervating and feminizing influences of the city. Or does the north begin at the 49th parallel separating Canada from its southern neighbour?

Sixty years ago, historian Arthur Lower said that the north begins where the pavement ends. Deliberately imprecise, he was hinting at something important: there are two norths. There is a real north, 'out there'. And there is an imagined north, 'in here'. An economic historian, Lower also understood that natural resources were 'out there' and that northern resource development was central to Canada's economic and national development.

Northern resource development

Founded in 1842, the Geological Survey of Canada confirmed what had been a dream since 1533 when Jacques Cartier was first instructed to find 'gold and other precious things' in the New World: the northern half of North America, far from being the land God gave to Cain, was one of the great geological prizes in world history. Across the second half of the 19th century and throughout the 20th century, its surveys, maps, and reports made northern resource development possible.

In 1887, for example, the Geological Survey mapped parts of northern British Columbia and the Yukon, an area it described as 'vast' and 'unknown'. It also confirmed reports of placer gold, or gold that can be recovered from gravel. Detailed and optimistic, the report quickly sold out and had to be reprinted; ten years later, it proved essential when the discovery of a large gold deposit in Rabbit Creek, a tributary of the Yukon's Klondike River, led to the Klondike gold rush in 1897–8. One estimate puts the number of men who undertook the impossible journey north at 100,000. Overnight, Dawson City—named in honour of George Dawson, who had led the 1887 survey—became the largest city west of Winnipeg.

The gold rush has inspired countless books and provided recurring stories to Canada's mythology, but, more importantly, it established a pattern that would endure for the next seventy-plus years: drawn into the informal labour market, Indigenous were also pushed to the margins of their traditional territories, hunting grounds, and trap lines. Confronted by the tragic introduction of disease, alcohol, and dependency, the Han in particular, 'the people of the river', became homeless in their own home and the gold rush became a defining event in their history. As well, the environmental footprint of the gold rush was enormous: forests were cut down; streams and creeks were rerouted; continuous fires were lit in mine shafts to melt the permafrost; tailings, or great heaps of rock and gravel, were left behind; and fish, bird, and wildlife habitats were ruined. But in 1900 almost no one used the language of destruction, although one or two commentators noted the ruthlessness of the miners. Instead, promoters and their politicians used the language of development and opportunity, of investment, extraction, transportation, markets, jobs, and profit: there was money to be made in Canada's norths.

However, northern resource development wouldn't be a game for men armed with shovels and a shared dream. It would be a game for companies armed with capital and powered by brute-force machines, the next larger than the last. Dotting the country from one end to the other, new mines were dug deep into the Laurentian Shield, a geological masterpiece of hard-rock minerals: nickel, silver, and gold in Sudbury, Cobalt, and Kirkland Lake, all in Ontario; iron ore in Schefferville and Labrador City along the Quebec–Labrador trough; copper, zinc, and gold in Flin Flon, Manitoba; uranium in Elliot Lake, Ontario, and McArthur River, Saskatchewan; lead and zinc in Nanisivik, Baffin Island; and, in the 1990s, diamonds near Lac de Gras, 300 kilometres north of Yellowknife and 200 kilometres south of the Arctic Circle. The assault on the forest, meanwhile, proceeded apace, now in the form of pulp and paper mills in nearly every province, from British Columbia to Newfoundland, to satiate the relentless demand for newsprint, especially in the United States. The *New York Times* turned the tiny settlement of Kapuskasing, Ontario, into a company town when it invested $30 million ($400 million today) in a mill that could produce 500 tonnes of newsprint every day. According to a 1931 description, Kapuskasing was a city dropped into Canada's north woods. A few years later, in 1936, the *Chicago Tribune* followed its rival's lead when it built Baie-Comeau, Quebec, a mill town on the north shore of the St Lawrence River. All of this, of course, required power. Decade over decade, northern rivers were dammed and hydroelectricity was generated with British Columbia, Ontario, and Quebec leading the way. By the end of the Second World War, Canada had become, according to one historian, a hydroelectric superpower. Across the next three decades, 600 more dams would be built. Tapping the north's wealth also required railways, highways, roadways, and even a seaway, the massive, multi-billion-dollar

St Lawrence Seaway, built by Canada and the United States in the 1950s. Connecting Canada's northern frontiers to markets in the United States, Europe, and Asia, and premised on commodity chains, backward and forward linkages, and capital accumulation, the new transportation routes have been described as corridors of modernization.

In the same way that the Klondike gold rush carried costs to the environment and Indigenous peoples, the uncountable development projects across northern Canada also carried costs, some truly heartbreaking. Located in northwestern Ontario, Dryden began as a mill town in the late 19th century, providing timber to the Canadian Pacific Railway. Early in the 20th century, a pulp mill opened and quickly became the region's principal economic driver, attracting workers and their families, as well as state officials and service providers. In many ways, Dryden was a successful resource town. But in 1962 the Reed Paper company began to dump 9,000 kilograms of mercury into the English–Wabigoon river system, poisoning the fish and, by extension, the community that caught them as a key part of its economy and diet: the Asupeeschoseewagong First Nation (Grassy Narrows). Although the mill stopped dumping mercury in 1970, incredibly, no clean-up was ordered by the government. As a result, the downstream effects on Grassy Narrows have been persistent and devastating: the rare cancers, cognitive impairments, neurological disorders, and developmental delays didn't go away and contributed to high rates of intergenerational alcoholism, violence, and suicide in what was, and is, a clear example of environmental racism and injustice. The people of Grassy Narrows fought back, using both the courts and direct action. In the meantime, promises were made and promises were broken. In 2014 a five-time chief of Grassy Narrows staged a hunger strike at Queen's Park, the Ontario legislature. Largely confined to a wheelchair, Steven Fobister wanted Ontario's decision makers to see first hand the effects of mercury poisoning. Although more promises were won, more delays were forthcoming. Finally, in 2018, the governments of Canada and Ontario committed to cleaning up the river and to building an on-site treatment centre. It would be too late for Fobister: he died a few weeks later, by then largely confined to a hospital bed.

Like the Laurentian Shield, the Western Canadian Sedimentary Basin is an enormous geomorphic region stretching up through the prairies to the Mackenzie Delta but, as a sedimentary basin, it contains vast reserves of oil and natural gas, not hard-rock minerals. When natural gas reserves were discovered in the Beaufort Sea in the late 1960s, plans were made to build a 1,200-kilometre pipeline that would follow the Mackenzie River, the longest river system in Canada, before connecting to existing pipelines in northern Alberta. As a northern resource development project, the Mackenzie Valley pipeline led to predictions of fantastic wealth. But it also raised difficult questions about the environment and equally difficult questions about the Indigenous peoples who called the Mackenzie Valley theirs, the Dene, Inuit, and Metis. In response, Ottawa appointed the Mackenzie Valley Pipeline Inquiry to be led by Justice Thomas Berger from the Supreme Court of British Columbia. For the next three years, Justice Berger spoke to industry experts and independent scientists who insisted that the project would not harm the environment and he listened to Indigenous peoples who insisted that the Mackenzie Valley was not a northern frontier but was their homeland and had been forever. In Old Crow, a small, fly-in Gwich'in community not far from the Bluefish Caves which are now thought to be the oldest sites of human occupation in northern North America, he met Alice Frost, who asked if white people had the right to ask them to give up their land, her question implying its own answer. 'You won't find many places like this left in the world,' she added.

Because he understood that Northrop Frye's void was Alice Frost's home, a humbled Justice Berger recommended in his 1977 report that any pipeline be delayed for at least ten years in order to resolve outstanding environmental questions and, crucially, to resolve outstanding land claims. Drawing on the experience of the Han people during the Klondike gold rush, he worried too about the social cost of rapid, large-scale development in the north, a cost always paid by Indigenous peoples. Hailed as a landmark in Canadian environmental awareness and in Indigenous–non-Indigenous relations, the Berger report effectively killed the pipeline when investors walked away. And going forward, it changed the rules of the game: northern development would require environmental impact assessments and meaningful Indigenous consultations. But it did not end the game. What Justice Berger identified as the logic of growth and 'the care and feeding of the industrial machine' weren't optional but were instead economic and political imperatives. Meeting those imperatives, capital and the state continued to move in tandem from one northern megaproject to the next: today, the natural resources sector constitutes 17 per cent of Canada's Gross Domestic Product and 47 per cent of its exports. The Mary River mine on Baffin Island, for example, now ships iron ore to a steel mill in Germany, 440 years after explorer Martin Frobisher returned to England with 1,000 tonnes of what he thought was gold but which turned out to be worthless Baffin Island rock.

Passionate about the north, Justice Berger referred to Canada's northern tradition and to Canadians as a northern people. It's the north, he said, that distinguishes Canada from the United States. Yet few Canadians live in the north, making the north an idea.

The north as an idea

Since the late 19th century, Canada has used the north as a symbol—in art, literature, music, humour, advertisements, and promotions—to define itself. Confederation-era politician George Alexander hoped that one day Canada would take its place among the nations of the world as a great northern power. Author Robert Grant Haliburton employed crude racial theories to argue that, because northern climates produce hardy and virtuous men with an instinct for freedom and for the rights of property, a great national spirit would be nurtured in what he called Canada's icy bosom. Robert Stanley Weir included a reference to 'The True North strong and free' in his patriotic song that became 'O Canada', the national anthem. In the 1920s and early 1930s the Group of Seven painted the north, literally from the near north to the far north, and, according to the mythology that quickly enveloped their work, painted a nation that extended from Canoe Lake north of Toronto to Ellesmere Island north of everything. Aware of their work and their intellectual project, Ottawa invited Group of Seven members A. Y. Jackson and Lawren Harris to accompany a 1930 Eastern Arctic Patrol in order to paint the Arctic and, crucially, to claim symbolic sovereignty over it. In the tradition of G. S. Nares, who claimed Ellesmere for Great Britain in 1875 when he planted a flag, and A. P. Low, who claimed Ellesmere for Canada in 1904 when he planted a flag (Figure 7), Jackson and Harris claimed Ellesmere when they painted it. Through our art, Jackson explained, 'we will get the Americans to think of the Arctic as part of Canada'.

And so it went: professional historian and amateur nationalist Donald Creighton called his 1944 history of Canada *Dominion of the North*; amateur historian and professional nationalist Pierre Berton published *The Mysterious North* in 1955; and producer turned nationalist Bernie Finklestein built True North Records with a mandate to record and distribute Canadian music by Canadian musicians. But northern nationalism could be a source of self-deprecating humour. Comedians Rick Moranis and Dave Thomas donned plaid shirts, tuques, and heavy winter coats in the 1980s to become Bob and Doug McKenzie, a couple of lovable hosers, Canadian slang for idiots, with their own talk show, *The Great White North*. At the same time, 'finding the Northwest Passage' became a Canadian euphemism for sex. Meanwhile, countless marketing campaigns have used northern tropes to sell everything from beer and chocolate to sex toys and equity funds,

7. In 1904, twenty-four years after acquiring the Arctic Archipelago, Canada sent an expedition to Ellesmere Island where A. P. Low and his men conducted their own act of occupation. As Low explained, 'a document taking formal possession in the name of King Edward VII, for the Dominion, was read, and the Canadian flag was raised and saluted'.

turning the north into a tired and overworked cliché. Indeed, a collection of Canadian zombie fiction billed itself as *Dead North* and featured the living dead dragging themselves across the icy tundra. For its part, the federal government built a $2 million 'fake lake'—with water, deck chairs, and iconic images of the Laurentian Shield—to market Canada's northern wilderness to the 2010 meeting of the G20, the group of nineteen industrialized countries plus the European Union. And yet, even if overworked, the north still works: in 2019 Toronto's professional basketball team, the Raptors, inspired Canadians on its championship run with its battle cry, 'We The North'.

Writers have used the north to explore a range of human emotions, from fear and loneliness to longing and nothingness.

In 'Death by Landscape', Margaret Atwood considers the enormity of Canada's near north, a place where a young girl can simply vanish off the edge of a cliff and disappear from time, swallowed by a massive and indifferent landscape. In 'Stone Mattress', she uses the far north as the perfect place to commit the perfect murder. In a barren landscape scarred by ancient glaciers and incised with intractable fjords, the main character asks, who will remember the man who raped her when they were both teenagers? For his part, singer-songwriter and Christian Bruce Cockburn cannot bear the thought of an indifferent universe where someone can never be found. In 'Northern Lights', he finds spiritual comfort in a night sky that seems to light the road to heaven. Poet Karen Connelly, however, doesn't find consolation, spiritual or otherwise, when she returns in winter to her childhood home on the prairies, a frozen world. Kneeling to kiss the ice, she cuts her lip.

Employed in journey novels—that is, novels premised on a journey to a specific place and an interior journey to one's self—the north functions as a site of exploration, redemption, or absolution. It can be a site too of fulfilment, even sexual fulfilment in the case of *Bear*, Marian Engel's controversial and explicit 1976 novel in which the main character leaves the south for the north, where she has an affair with a bear, an actual affair with an actual bear. Or it can be a site of feminist reclamation. In *Places Far From Ellesmere*, Aritha van Herk un-writes Ellesmere Island as a place of male expedition and conquest and rewrites it as a place of female possibility and emancipation.

In 2016 the Art Gallery of Ontario held a special exhibition entitled 'The Idea of the North: The Paintings of Lawren Harris'. As part of the exhibition, the AGO provided an activity book to children, asking them to identify some things and to colour other things. They were also invited to write down what the north meant to them, which the Gallery would add to its wall of ideas: Canadians are not born northern, they are made northern.

But who, exactly, are Canadians? After all, Quebec too sees itself through its north, also geographically indeterminate and also invented: the boreal cold and sombre northern nights in Louis Fréchette's epic poem, *La Légende d'un peuple*; the depictions of winter life in the paintings of Cornelius Krieghoff; and the images of history, memory, people, and winter in the paintings of Jean Paul Lemieux. 'Mon pays', a 1964 song by Gilles Vigneault, captured what it meant to be Québécois. *Mon pays, ce n'est pas un pays, c'est l'hiver*, he wrote. My country isn't a country, it's winter. Fearing that 'Mon pays', now a Quebec folk anthem, would be played against the Canadian flag, Vigneault refused to let the 2010 Vancouver winter Olympics use it in the opening ceremonies.

Quebec even has its own word to describe its northern identity. Invented in the 1960s, *nordicité* originally referred to a location's degree of northernness as measured by such objective criteria as latitude, temperature, and snowfall. But in the Quiet Revolution and the remaking of Quebec nationalism, it became a convenient shorthand for a fundamental aspect of Quebec's national identity. In 2005 the news magazine *L'actualité* included nordicity, in addition to cold and winter, in its list of 101 words that describe Quebec. And in 2012 the Montreal-based hipster magazine of pop cult *Urbania* dedicated an entire issue to the celebration of winter as a celebration of Quebecers as a people. Of course, Quebecers have been celebrating winter for a long time. In the late 19th century Montreal and Quebec organized fantastic carnivals to transform the cold into a virtue and to attract tourists, although it wasn't until 1955 that the Quebec Winter Carnival became a permanent fixture of the Quebec calendar or that its snowman mascot, Bonhomme Carnaval, became an instantly recognizable symbol of Quebec, his red tuque and arrow sash channelling Quebec's northern history.

It was that history that the Parti Québécois wanted to summon in the 1995 referendum. The long preamble to Bill 1 that established the legal framework for sovereignty deliberately linked Quebec's winter, its 'false eternity' and its 'apparent deaths', whatever they are, to Quebec's independence: 'We know the winter in our souls.'

To fill Northrop Frye's void and, although they would reject this assertion, to claim Alice Frost's home as theirs, English Canadians and Quebecers have used their respective great white norths as great white sheets on which to write their emotions and their fantasies, both individual and national. Quebec poet Pierre Morency once said that 'le nord n'est pas dans la boussole il est ici'. The north isn't in the compass it's here. Governor General Adrienne Clarkson often quoted Morency, the image speaking to her intuitive understanding of Canada. When she made the north a theme of her tenure, no one was surprised: what could be more Canadian than the Queen's representative sleeping in an igloo, riding a dog sled, and ice fishing?

Because the north is so intimately connected to who Canadians are, Clarkson said in 2003, for Canadians to deny the north is to engage in a form of self-contempt. But to accept uncritically the north as something that will always be there is to engage in a form of self-delusion: climate change is changing the north in irreversible ways.

Climate change, climate politics, and Arctic sovereignty

Climate science was in its infancy in 1977 when Justice Berger wondered what an oil spill in the Beaufort Sea would mean for the albedo, or the reflective capacity, of the sea ice. Sea ice with a diminished albedo would reflect less light and melt more quickly, he said, thereby enlarging the area of open water and, potentially, lengthening the duration of open water. Given that sea ice is the thermostat for the northern hemisphere, could it bring about changes in the climate? he asked. The scientists didn't think so, but also conceded their uncertainty. Berger let the question drop, saying that it lay 'far in the future'.

Anthropogenic climate change—defined as global heating caused by the accumulation in the atmosphere of greenhouse gases (GHGs) that trap infrared radiation, or heat—has had, and will have, lasting consequences for Canada in general and the Arctic in particular. A complicated phenomenon called polar amplification means that the Arctic is heating at twice the rate of the global average and that, in turn, means shrinking sea ice, melting glaciers, and thawing permafrost. A remarkable 50 per cent of Canada is permafrost, making Canada not a hockey nation, but a permafrost nation. Trapped in the permafrost are carbon dioxide and methane that are released when the permafrost thaws, creating a feedback loop in which warming leads to more warming. As climate scientists often say, what happens in the Arctic doesn't stay in the Arctic because changes to the extent and thickness of sea ice will alter hemispheric climates and weather patterns over the short and long terms. Predicting rates of warming and rates of summer sea ice loss is not easy, but researchers believe that the Arctic Ocean will see ice-free summers by 2040, if not 2030.

Because of its historical commitment to multilateralism and to the United Nations, Canada ratified the Kyoto Protocol—or Kyoto for short—in 2002. Taking steps to mitigate climate change confirmed Canada's self-image as a middle-power boy scout doing the right thing. However, Canada didn't acknowledge that Kyoto's targets were weak because of its behind-the-scenes efforts with Japan, the United States, Australia, Norway, and New Zealand to ensure an unambitious and therefore inexpensive treaty. And yet Canada still couldn't meet its Kyoto targets. Reluctant to impose any kind of meaningful caps on industrial GHG emissions, or to retard northern resource development, especially Alberta's oil sands, it embraced instead a neo-liberal solution when it put the onus of emissions reduction on the individual, inviting Canadians to reduce their carbon footprint by changing their light bulbs, taking public transportation, and buying energy-efficient appliances. Despite high-minded promises from successive governments to find a made-in-Canada solution to emissions instead of a made-in-Japan solution, only a handful of policies were implemented, and those tended to be at the sub-national level by provinces and municipalities. Emissions, meanwhile, continued to rise and, in 2012, Canada formally withdrew from Kyoto.

In 2015 the Liberal government of Justin Trudeau signed the Paris Agreement and committed to a series of climate policies taking collective aim at Canada's Paris goal. The most ambitious policy, and therefore the most controversial, was the 2019 carbon price, or tax, to be paid by consumers, businesses, and industry. A market signal designed to discourage consumption and to encourage conservation and green investment, the carbon price, while laudable, is too little, too late. Part of the problem is Paris itself. An anaemic agreement, it makes an incredible confession when, in diplomatic language, it 'notes with concern' that country targets, now called contributions, are not enough to meet the agreement's goal of holding the increase in global average temperature to well below 2° Celsius. Part of the problem too is Canada's deep economic integration with the United States: the continental straitjacket being what it is, Canada cannot impose a steep carbon price on its exports to a country that has withdrawn from Paris. But the real problem is the logic of economic growth. Unable to think outside of that logic, Ottawa undermined its climate agenda when, in 2019, it committed to twinning the Trans Mountain pipeline to carry oil from Alberta to marine terminals in British Columbia for sale in Asian energy markets. Justice Berger identified the logic of growth as the care and feeding of the industrial machine. Forty-plus years later, environmentalist David Suzuki called it a form of brain damage.

Climate change is also bringing a fresh urgency to an old question: Arctic sovereignty. No one questions Canada's sovereignty over the Arctic Archipelago. But the Northwest Passage is different. Canada insists that it lies in internal waters. But the United States contends that it lies in international waters, a debate complicated by the fact that the passage is not one route but four with another four secondary routes. Likewise, the exact limits of the continental shelves stretching along the floor of the Arctic Ocean from Canada, the United States, Greenland (Denmark), Norway, and Russia remain uncertain and contested. Where does one shelf end and another shelf begin? If the question is legal, technical, and inching its way through the United Nations Convention on the Law of the Sea, it's also political, commercial, and making its way across the Arctic through oil and gas exploration. No one knows how much oil and natural gas is trapped beneath the ice, but some estimates suggest that 13 per cent of the world's undiscovered oil reserves and 30 per cent of the world's undiscovered natural gas reserves may lie at the bottom of the Arctic Ocean. Since the early 2000s, Canada has sought to reassert its Arctic sovereignty and in 2017 it opened the $250 million Canadian High Arctic Research Station in Cambridge Bay, Nunavut, a year-round research facility to support Arctic science, including climate science.

When the Toronto *Globe* announced in 1880 that Canada extended from ocean to ocean to ocean, it also reported that the Arctic was of 'little value'. Of course, that was never the case and it certainly isn't the case today. Chasing the next windfall, and fuelled by the prospect of ice-free summers, the world's Arctic powers are engaged in a Klondike-like rush to stake their claims to oil and gas reserves that may, or may not, lead to an Arctic bonanza. After all, the challenges of distance and of technology are considerable. But that countries are even talking about a fossil fuel bonanza at the top of the world is astounding to climate researchers who continue to document the impacts of climate change in the Arctic. The only surprise is the rapidity of change, including on Ellesmere Island: ice cap melt on the Hazen Plateau; permafrost thaw, terrain subsidence, and carbon release on the Fosheim Peninsula; and ice calves falling from the Ward Hunt Ice Shelf, described by the 1875–6 Nares expedition as 'a long fringe of large and troublesome hummocks', or ice hills that resemble steep mountain peaks.

If Canada's real north, the one 'out there', is changing, so too is its imagined north, the one 'in here'. In 'Arctic Dreams', poet Sue Sinclair admits that as a suburban kid she grew up with the idea of the north and felt protected by it, not haunted by it like Northrop Frye. But her response now to watching calved ice float into a 'motherless distance' isn't protection. It's fear.

Conclusion

This book ends where it began, with the Syrian diaspora and the arrival of 60,000 Syrian refugees beginning in late 2015. After four years, they have learned one of Canada's two official languages, enrolled their children in schools, colleges, and universities, entered the labour market, and, in some instances, opened businesses. The latest in a long line of immigrants and refugees, they are contributing to their new home and confirming its commitment to pluralism.

To prepare for their citizenship test, Qassim Albrdan and Manal Hredeen read *Discover Canada: The Rights and Responsibilities of Citizenship*, the official citizenship study guide that introduces new Canadians to their new country. Starting with Indigenous peoples, New France, and British North America, *Discover Canada* moves quickly across time and space, emphasizing Canada's military history, from the Plains of Abraham and the War of 1812 to the Western Front, D-Day, and Kandahar. It includes residential schools, Quebec nationalism, multiculturalism, and the struggle for women's rights and gay and lesbian rights. And it gives shout-outs to the world's longest undefended border, peacekeeping, and Arctic sovereignty. But *Discover Canada* excludes labour and labour history, a subject marginalized by neo-liberalism's commitment to unorganized and precarious work. As a result, the Albrdans didn't learn about

8. **Syrian refugee Mohammad Nour Albrdan proudly wears a very Canadian T-shirt featuring a red maple leaf and the word 'Eh?' Used to confirm a statement—as in, 'Nice day, eh?'—'eh' distinguishes Canadian English from American English and thus English Canadians from Americans.**

organized labour's historical struggle for the right to collective bargaining and the right to strike.

Discover Canada succeeded nonetheless in its assigned task because the Albrdans were genuinely excited by Canada's history, proudly recounting facts, figures, and the name of Canada's first prime minister, Sir John A. Macdonald: you can't belong to a country unless you know something about that country (Figure 8). But *Discover Canada* started from the assumption that there is a single Canada. This Very Short Introduction started from a different premise when it selected six words and quickly pluralized them: beginning became beginnings, nationalism became nationalisms, and so on. Geographically large, historically complicated, and made up of people from around the world, Canada can't be reduced to a common denominator because there isn't one. And that is a good thing.

References

Chapter 1: Beginnings

Jacques Cartier. Quotations in Ramsay Cook, ed., *The Voyages of Jacques Cartier* (Toronto: University of Toronto Press, 1993), 10, 24, 26, 38, 9.

Voyages of Samuel de Champlain (Raleigh, NC: Hayes Barton Press, 2005), 36, 196.

Jacques Cartier. Quotation in Cook, *The Voyages of Jacques Cartier*, 21.

Afua Cooper, 'Confessions of a Woman Who Burnt Down a Town', in Afua Cooper, ed., *Utterances and Incantations: Women, Poetry, and Dub* (Toronto: Sister Vision Press, 1999), 84.

Ojibwa chief Minweweh. Quotation in Olive Patricia Dickason with David T. McNab, *Canada's First Nations: A History of Founding Peoples from Earliest Times*, 4th edn (Toronto: Oxford University Press, 2009), 151.

Newspaper quotations in P. B. Waite, *The Life and Times of Confederation, 1864–1867: Politics, Newspapers, and the Union of British North America* (Toronto: University of Toronto Press, 1962), 322.

Chapter 2: Dispossessions

Treaty 6 between Her Majesty the Queen and the Plain and Wood Cree Indians, 1876. Available at <https://www.aadnc-aandc.gc.ca/eng/1100100028710/1100100028783>.

M. C. Cameron, Debates, House of Commons, 15 April 1886.

One Arrow. Quotation in Rudy Wiebe, *Big Bear* (Toronto: Penguin, 2008), 191.

Final Statement of Louis Riel, 31 July 1885. Available at <http://www.famous-trials.com/louisriel/859-statement>.

Honouring the Truth, Reconciling the Future: Summary of the Final Report of the Truth and Reconciliation Commission of Canada (Ottawa, 2015), 3.

Joseph Auguste Merasty, with David Carpenter, *The Education of Augie Merasty: A Residential School Memoir* (Regina: University of Regina Press, 2015), 16.

Duncan Campbell Scott. Quotation in John S. Milloy, *A National Crime: The Canadian Government and the Residential School System* (Winnipeg: University of Manitoba Press, 1999), 46.

Sandra Lovelace. Additional Information and Observations Drafted by Mrs Sandra Lovelace, 20 June 1980. Available at <http://www.usask.ca/nativelaw/unhrfn/lovelacefiles/doc14.pdf>.

Chapter 3: Nationalisms

William Black Creighton, *Christian Guardian*, 26 August 1914.

Henri Bourassa. Quotation in Joseph Levitt, ed., *Henri Bourassa on Imperialism and Biculturalism, 1900–1918* (Toronto: Copp Clark, 1970), 64.

Hugh MacLennan, *Scotchman's Return and Other Essays* (New York: Scribner's, 1960), 113.

Pierre Trudeau, Debates, House of Commons, 8 October 1971.

1987 Constitutional Accord. Available at: <https://www.canada.ca/en/intergovernmental-affairs/services/federation/1987-constitutional-accord.html>.

Chapter 4: Rights

Lord Durham's Report on the Affairs of British North America, 1839 (Oxford: Clarendon, 1912), 236.

R v. *Morgentaler*, 1988, Supreme Court of Canada, 172.

Egan v. *Canada*, 1995, Supreme Court of Canada, 514.

Act Respecting the Laicity of the State 2019, Preamble.

Health Services and Support-Facilities Subsector Bargaining Assn v. *British Columbia*, 2007, Supreme Court of Canada, para. 82.

Saskatchewan Federation of Labour v. *Saskatchewan*, 2015, Supreme Court of Canada, para. 3.

Canada

Chapter 5: Borders

Pierre Elliott Trudeau, *Conversation with Canadians* (Toronto: University of Toronto Press, 1972), 174.

Jack Granatstein, *How Britain's Weakness Forced Canada into the Arms of the United States* (Toronto: University of Toronto Press, 1989), 11.

Margaret Atwood, 'Blind Faith and Free Trade', in Ralph Nader et al., *The Case Against 'Free Trade': GATT, NAFTA, and the Globalization of Corporate Greed* (San Francisco: Earth Island Press, 1993), 94.

'Let loose the war on global terrorism', *Globe and Mail*, 12 September 2001.

Foreign Policy for Canadians (Ottawa: Department of External Affairs, 1970), 21.

Chapter 6: Norths

Report on an Exploration in the Yukon District, N.W.T., and Adjacent Northern Portion of British Columbia, 1887 (Ottawa: Geological Survey of Canada, 1887), 6.

Northern Frontier, Northern Homeland: Report of the Mackenzie Valley Pipeline Inquiry, vol. 1 (Ottawa, 1977), 38.

Thomas Berger, 'The Mackenzie Valley Pipeline Inquiry', *Osgoode Hall Law Journal*, 16, 3 (1978), 646.

A. Y. Jackson. Quotation in Agnes Ladon, 'Art and Arctic Sovereignty: A. Y. Jackson and Lawren S. Harris and Canada's Eastern Arctic Patrols', Queen's University, MA Thesis, 2012.

Bill 1, An Act Respecting the Future of Quebec (Quebec, 1995).

Pierre Morency, 'lieu de naissance', in Pierre Morency, *A Season for Birds: Selected Poems* (Toronto: Exile, 1990), 56.

Northern Frontier, Northern Homeland, 1:xvii.

Toronto *Globe*, 11 October 1880.

G. S. Nares, *Narrative of a Voyage to the Polar Sea* (London, 1878), 356.

Sue Sinclair, 'Arctic Dreams', 2018. Unpublished.

Further reading

General

Dimitry Anastakis, *Re-Creation, Fragmentation, and Resilience: A Brief History of Canada since 1945* (Don Mills, Ontario: Oxford University Press, 2018).

Jeanette Armstrong and Lally Grauer, eds, *Native Poetry in Canada: A Contemporary Anthology* (Peterborough: Broadview, 2001).

Gail Cuthbert Brandt et al., *Canadian Women: A History*, 3rd edn (Toronto: Nelson, 2011).

Sean Cadigan, *Newfoundland and Labrador: A History* (Toronto: University of Toronto Press, 2009).

Colin M. Coates and Graeme Wynn, eds, *The Nature of Canada* (Vancouver: UBC Press, 2019).

Margaret Conrad, *A Concise History of Canada* (Cambridge: Cambridge University Press, 2012).

Michael Dawson et al., *Symbols of Canada* (Toronto: Between the Lines, 2018).

Olive Patricia Dickason and William Newbigging, *Indigenous Peoples within Canada*, 4th edn (Don Mills, Ontario: Oxford University Press, 2018).

John Dickinson and Brian Young, *A Short History of Quebec*, 4th edn (Montreal and Kingston: McGill-Queen's University Press, 2008).

Marlene Epp, *Refugees in Canada: A Brief History* (Ottawa: Canadian Historical Association, 2017).

J. L. Granatstein, *Canada's Army: Waging War and Keeping the Peace*, 2nd edn (Toronto: University of Toronto Press, 2011).

Coral Ann Howells and Eva-Marie Kröller, eds, *The Cambridge History of Canadian Literature* (Cambridge: Cambridge University Press, 2009).

Ninette Kelly and Michael Trebilcock, *The Making of the Mosaic: A History of Canadian Immigration Policy*, 2nd edn (Toronto: University of Toronto Press, 2010).

Mary-Ellen Kelm and Lorna Townsend, eds, *In the Days of our Grandmothers: A Reader in Aboriginal Women's History in Canada* (Toronto: University of Toronto Press, 2006).

John Sutton Lutz, *Makúk: A New History of Aboriginal-White Relations* (Vancouver: UBC Press, 2009).

Laurel Sefton MacDowell, *An Environmental History of Canada* (Toronto: University of Toronto Press, 2008).

J. R. Miller, *Skyscrapers Hide the Heavens: A History of Native-Newcomer Relations in Canada*, 4th edn (Toronto: University of Toronto Press, 2018).

Desmond Morton, *A Military History of Canada*, 5th edn (Toronto: McClelland and Stewart, 2007).

Chapter 1: Beginnings

Phillip Buckner and John G. Reid, eds, *Remembering 1759: The Conquest of Canada in Historical Memory* (Toronto: University of Toronto Press, 2012).

Ramsay Cook, *1492 and All That: Making a Garden out of a Wilderness* (Toronto: York University Robarts Centre for Canadian Studies, 1996).

Afua Cooper, *The Hanging of Angélique: The Untold Story of Canadian Slavery and the Burning of Montreal* (Toronto: HarperCollins, 2006).

Olive Patricia Dickason, *The Myth of the Savage: And the Beginnings of French Colonialism in the Americas* (Edmonton: University of Alberta Press, 1984).

Michel Ducharme, *The Idea of Liberty in Canada during the Age of Atlantic Revolutions, 1776-1838*, trans. Peter Feldstein (Montreal and Kingston: McGill-Queen's University Press, 2014).

Allan Greer, *Peasant, Lord, and Merchant: Rural Society in Three Quebec Parishes, 1740-1840* (Toronto: University of Toronto Press, 1985).

Allan Greer, *The People of New France* (Toronto: University of Toronto Press, 1997).

Cole Harris, *The Reluctant Land: Society, Space, and Environment in Canada before Confederation* (Vancouver: UBC Press, 2009).

Norman Knowles, *Inventing the Loyalists: The Ontario Loyalist Tradition and the Creation of Usable Pasts* (Toronto: University of Toronto Press, 1997).

Jacqueline Krikorian et al., *Roads to Confederation: The Making of Canada, 1867*, 2 vols (Toronto: University of Toronto Press, 2017).

Ged Martin, *John A. Macdonald: Canada's First Prime Minister* (Toronto: Dundurn, 2013).

Carolyn Produchny, *Making the Voyageur World: Travelers and Traders in the North American Fur Trade* (Lincoln, Neb.: University of Nebraska Press and Toronto: University of Toronto Press, 2007).

Bruce Trigger, *Natives and Newcomers: Canada's 'Heroic Age' Reconsidered* (Montreal and Kingston: McGill-Queen's University Press, 1985).

Sylvia Van Kirk, *Many Tender Ties: Women in Fur-Trade Society, 1670–1870* (Norman, Okla.: University of Oklahoma Press, 1983).

John Weaver, *The Great Land Rush and the Making of the Modern World* (Montreal and Kingston: McGill-Queen's University Press, 2003).

Harvey Amani Whitfield, *North to Bondage: Loyalist Slavery in the Maritimes* (Vancouver: UBC Press, 2016).

Chapter 2: Dispossessions

Albert Braz, *The False Traitor: Louis Riel in Canadian Culture* (Toronto: University of Toronto Press, 2003).

Sarah Carter, *Lost Harvests: Prairie Indian Reserve Farmers and Government Policy* (Montreal and Kingston: McGill-Queen's University Press, 1990).

James Daschuck, *Clearing the Plains: Disease, Politics of Starvation, and the Loss of Aboriginal Life* (Regina: University of Regina Press, 2013).

Shelley A. M. Gavigan, *Hunger, Horses, and Government Men: Criminal Law on the Aboriginal Plains, 1870–1905* (Vancouver: UBC Press, 2013).

Andrew C. Isenberg, *The Destruction of the Bison: An Environmental History, 1750–1920* (Cambridge: Cambridge University Press, 2000).

Mary-Ellen Kelm, *Colonizing Bodies: Aboriginal Health and Healing in British Columbia, 1900–1950* (Vancouver: UBC Press, 1999).

Mary-Ellen Kelm and Keith D. Smith, *Talking Back to the Indian Act: Critical Readings in Settler Colonial Histories* (Toronto: University of Toronto Press, 2018).

Mary-Jane Logan McCallum, *Indigenous Women, Work, and History, 1940–1980* (Winnipeg: University of Manitoba Press, 2014).

J. R. Miller, *Shingwauk's Vision: A History of Native Residential Schools* (Toronto: University of Toronto Press, 1996).

Sarah Nickel, 'Reconsidering 1969: The *White Paper* and the Making of the Modern Indigenous Rights Movement', *Canadian Historical Review* 100, 2 (June 2019), 223–38.

Blair Stonechild and Bill Waiser, *Loyal Till Death: Indians and the North-West Rebellion* (Calgary: Fifth House, 1997).

Chapter 3: Nationalisms

Catherine Annau, dir., *Just Watch Me* (National Film Board of Canada, 1999).

Michael Behiels, *Prelude to Quebec's Quiet Revolution: Liberalism vs Neo-Nationalism, 1945–1960* (Montreal and Kingston: McGill-Queen's University Press, 1985).

Carl Berger, *Sense of Power: Studies in the Ideas of Canadian Imperialism, 1867–1914*, 2nd edn (Toronto: University of Toronto Press, 2013).

Philip Buckner, *Canada and the End of Empire* (Vancouver: UBC Press, 2004).

Philip Buckner and R. Douglas Francis, eds, *Canada and the British World: Culture, Migration, and Identity* (Vancouver: UBC Press, 2006).

Ramsay Cook, *Canada, Quebec, and the Uses of Nationalism*, 2nd edn (Toronto: McClelland and Stewart, 1995).

John English, *Citizen of the World: The Life of Pierre Elliott Trudeau, 1919–1968* and *Just Watch Me: The Life of Pierre Elliott Trudeau, 1968–2000* (Toronto: Vintage, 2007, 2010).

Norman Hillmer and Adam Chapnick, eds, *Canadas of the Mind: The Making and Unmaking of Canadian Nationalisms in the Twentieth Century* (Montreal and Kingston: McGill-Queen's University Press, 2007).

José Igartua, *The Other Quiet Revolution: National Identities in English Canada, 1945–1971* (Vancouver: UBC Press, 2009).

Paul Litt, *Trudeaumania* (Vancouver: UBC Press, 2016).

Bryan D. Palmer, *Canada's 1960s: The Ironies of Identities in a Rebellious Era* (Toronto: University of Toronto Press, 2009).

Peter Russell, *Constitutional Odyssey: Can Canadians Become a Sovereign People?*, 3rd edn (Toronto: University of Toronto Press, 2004).

Robert Wright, *The Night Canada Stood Still: How the 1995 Referendum Nearly Cost Us our Country* (Toronto: HarperCollins, 2014).

Chapter 4: Rights

David Bedford, 'Emancipation as Oppression: The Marshall Decision and Self-Government', *Journal of Canadian Studies* 44, 1 (2010), 206–20.

Michael Behiels, *Canada's Francophone Minority Communities: Constitutional Renewal and the Winning of School Governance* (Montreal and Kingston: McGill-Queen's University Press, 2005).

Gérard Bouchard, *Interculturalism: A View from Quebec*, trans. Howard Scott (Toronto: University of Toronto Press, 2015).

David Calverley, *Who Controls the Hunt? First Nations, Treaty Rights, and Wildlife Conservation in Ontario, 1783–1939* (Vancouver: UBC Press, 2018).

Dominique Clément, *Canada's Rights Revolution: Social Movements and Social Change, 1937–1982* (Vancouver: UBC Press, 2008).

David Frank, *J. B. McLachlan: A Biography* (Toronto: Lorimer, 1999).

Rachael Johnstone, *After Morgentaler: The Politics of Abortion in Canada* (Vancouver: UBC Press, 2018).

Gregory S. Kealey and Bryan D. Palmer, *Dreaming of What Might Be: The Knights of Labor in Ontario, 1880–1900* (New York: Cambridge University Press, 1982).

Valerie Korinek, *Prairie Fairies: A History of Queer Communities and People in Western Canada, 1930–1985* (Toronto: University of Toronto Press, 2018).

Christopher MacLennan, *Toward the Charter: Canada and the Demand for a National Bill of Rights, 1929–1960* (Montreal and Kingston: McGill-Queen's University Press, 2003).

Carmela Patrias and Ruth Frager, *Discounted Labour: Women Workers in Canada, 1870–1939* (Toronto: University of Toronto Press, 2005).

Arthur J. Ray, *Aboriginal Rights Claims and the Making and Remaking of History* (Montreal and Kingston: McGill-Queen's University Press, 2016).

Larry Savage and Charles Smith, *Unions in Court: Organized Labour and the Charter of Rights and Freedoms* (Vancouver: UBC Press, 2017).

Christabelle Sethna and Steve Hewitt, *Just Watch Us: RCMP Surveillance of the Women's Liberation Movement in Cold War Canada* (Montreal and Kingston: McGill-Queen's University Press, 2018).

Miriam Smith, *Lesbian and Gay Rights in Canada: Social Movements and Equality Seeking, 1971–1995* (Toronto: University of Toronto Press, 1999).

Shannon Stettner et al., *Abortion: History, Politics, and Reproductive Justice after Morgentaler* (Vancouver: UBC Press, 2018).

Robert C. Vipond, *Making a Global City: How One Toronto School Embraced Diversity* (Toronto: University of Toronto Press, 2017).

Tom Warner, *Never Going Back: A History of Queer Activism in Canada* (Toronto: University of Toronto Press, 2002).

Reg Whitaker et al., *Secret Service: Political Policing in Canada from the Fenians to Fortress America* (Toronto: University of Toronto Press, 2012).

Chapter 5: Borders

Raymond Blake, *Transforming the Nation: Canada and Brian Mulroney* (Montreal and Kingston: McGill-Queen's University Press, 2007).

Robert Bothwell, *Alliance and Illusion: Canada and the World, 1945–1984* (Vancouver: UBC Press, 2008).

Jean-Christophe Boucher and Kim Nossal, *The Politics of War: Canada's Afghanistan Mission, 2001–2014* (Vancouver: UBC Press, 2017).

Francis M. Carroll, *A Good and Wise Measure: The Search for the Canadian–American Boundary, 1783–1842* (Toronto: University of Toronto Press, 2001).

Adam Chapnick, *The Middle Power Project: Canada and the Founding of the United Nations* (Vancouver: UBC Press, 2005).

Matthew Evenden, *Allied Power: Mobilizing Hydro-electricity during Canada's Second World War* (Toronto: University of Toronto Press, 2015).

J. L. Granatstein, *Yankee Go Home? Canadians and Anti-Americanism* (Toronto: HarperCollins, 1997).

Norman Hillmer and J. L. Granatstein, *For Better or for Worse: Canada and the United States into the Twenty-First Century* (Toronto: Thomson Nelson, 2007).

Colin McCullough and Robert Teigrob, eds, *Canada and the United Nations: Legacies, Limits, Prospects* (Montreal and Kingston: McGill-Queen's University Press, 2016).

Bruce Muirhead, *Dancing Around the Elephant: Creating a Prosperous Canada in an Era of American Dominance, 1957–1973* (Toronto: University of Toronto Press, 2007).

Philip Resnick, *Letters to a Québécois Friend* (Montreal and Kingston: McGill-Queen's University Press, 1990).

John Herd Thompson and Stephen J. Randall, *Canada and the United States: Ambivalent Allies*, 3rd edn (Athens, Ga: University of Georgia Press, 2002).

Lee Windsor et al., *Kandahar Tour: The Turning Point in Canada's Afghan Mission* (Fredericton: Gregg Centre for the Study of War and Society, 2008).

Chapter 6: Norths

Margaret Atwood, *Strange Things: The Malevolent North in Canadian Literature* (Oxford: Clarendon Press, 1995).

Robert Bone, *The Canadian North: Issues and Challenges*, 4th edn (Don Mills, Ontario: Oxford University Press, 2012).

Janice Cavell and Jeff Noakes, *Acts of Occupation: Canada and Arctic Sovereignty, 1918–1925* (Vancouver: UBC Press, 2011).

Kenneth Coates and William Robert Morrison, *Land of the Midnight Sun: A History of the Yukon* (Montreal and Kingston: McGill-Queen's University Press, 2005).

Sherill Grace, *Canada and the Idea of North* (Montreal and Kingston: McGill-Queen's University Press, 2007).

Shelagh Grant, *A History of Arctic Sovereignty in North America* (Vancouver: Douglas and McIntyre, 2010).

Renée Hulan, *Northern Experience and the Myths of Canadian Culture* (Montreal and Kingston: McGill-Queen's University Press, 2002).

Liza Piper, *The Industrial Transformation of Subarctic Canada* (Vancouver: UBC Press, 2009).

Graeme Wynn, *Canada and Arctic North America: An Environmental History* (Santa Barbara, Calif.: ABC-CLIO, 2007).

Morris Zaslow, ed., *A Century of Canada's Arctic Islands, 1880–1980* (Ottawa: Royal Society of Canada, 1981).

Canada

Publisher's acknowledgements

We are grateful for permission to include the following copyright material in this book.

Extract from 'Confessions of a Woman Who Burnt Down a Town', in Afua Cooper, ed., *Utterances and Incantations: Women, Poetry, and Dub* (Toronto: Sister Vision Press, 1999), 84. Used with permission.

'American Woman', Words & Music by Jim Kale, Randy Bachman, Garry Peterson & Burton Cummings. © Copyright 1988 Shillelagh America Music. BMG Rights Management (US) LLC. All Rights Reserved. International Copyright Secured. Used by permission of Hal Leonard Europe Limited.

Extract from 'Mon Pays' © Gilles Vigneault/David Murphy et Cie.

Extract from Pierre Morency, *A Season for Birds: Selected Poems*, trans. Alexandre L. Ampromoz (Toronto: Exile, 1990), p. 56. Used by permission.

Extract from Sue Sinclair, 'Arctic Dreams', unpublished.

Index

For the benefit of digital users, indexed terms that span two pages
(e.g., 52–53) may, on occasion, appear on only one of those pages.

Canada

MODERN CHINA
A Very Short Introduction
Rana Mitter

China today is never out of the news: from human rights
controversies and the continued legacy of Tiananmen Square,
to global coverage of the Beijing Olympics, and the Chinese
'economic miracle'. It seems a country of contradictions: a
peasant society with some of the world's most futuristic cities,
heir to an ancient civilization that is still trying to find a modern
identity. This *Very Short Introduction* offers the reader with no
previous knowledge of China a variety of ways to understand
the world's most populous nation, giving a short, integrated
picture of modern Chinese society, culture, economy, politics
and art.

'A brilliant essay.'

Timothy Garton, TLS

www.oup.com/vsi

MODERN JAPAN
A Very Short Introduction
Christopher Goto-Jones

Japan is arguably today's most successful industrial economy,
combining almost unprecedented affluence with social stability
and apparent harmony. Japanese goods and cultural products
are consumed all over the world, ranging from animated
movies and computer games all the way through to cars,
semiconductors, and management techniques. In many ways,
Japan is an icon of the modern world, and yet it remains
something of an enigma to many, who see it as a confusing
montage of the alien and the familiar, the ancient and modern.
The aim of this Very Short Introduction is to explode the myths
and explore the reality of modern Japan - by taking a concise
look at its history, economy, politics, and culture.

'A wonderfully engaging narrative of a complicated history, which
from the beginning to end sheds light on the meaning of modernity
in Japan as it changed over time. An exemplary text.'

Carol Gluck, Columbia University